Complete instruction in Rearing Silkworms

Carrie Williams

BIBLIOLIFE

COMPLETE INSTRUCTION

IN

REARING SILKWORMS

ALSO

HOW TO BUILD AND FURNISH COCOONERIES

HOW TO PLANT, PRUNE, AND CARE
FOR MULBERRY TREES

TOGETHER WITH

MUCH VALUABLE INFORMATION AS TO THE SILK
INDUSTRY IN GENERAL

BY

MRS. CARRIE WILLIAMS
Sericulturist

SAN FRANCISCO
THE WHITAKER AND RAY COMPANY
(INCORPORATED)
1902

PREFACE.

In sending out this little volume to the American public, I do so with the earnest hope of calling attention to this very important branch of industry.

Close study and observation on practical lines for more than ten years gives me confidence to assert that no one factor in the industrial interests of our nation is of greater importance than is the production of silk, and yet there is none so little understood, and hence so lightly valued.

The wealth of every nation lies in its developed resources. We might build castles of stone upon mountains of gold, but the gold, though of greater intrinsic value, would be no better than (if as good) the stone employed in the superstructure of the building.

Wealth, in order to be helpful, either to the individual or the nation, must be developed; otherwise it will forever remain like the talent folded away in the napkin

Knowing that a want of knowledge of the silk business has caused so many failures with those who, from time to time, have attempted silk-culture in this country, I send out this book with full instructions, which I know, if strictly followed, will insure success.

By contrasting our advantages, as set forth in these pages, with other countries, it will readily be seen that *everything* is in our favor, save only education,—experience, which might very soon be acquired, and that, too, on a much higher plane than that on which nine tenths of the silk of the world is produced.

We need not content ourselves with doing as well as others have done. We can do *better*.

In the manufacture of silk we captured the highest premiums from the whole world at the Paris Exposition in A. D. 1900. Yet there are no special advantages here for the manufacture of silk, more than in any country from which we import reeled silk and also manufactured goods. But we have here very many special advantages for the production of silk, and with the hope, in some measure, of waking up the people at large to avail themselves of the great advantages we enjoy, and the grand possibilities to which we might attain, I now send forth this little book upon the sea of ever-expanding literature of the twentieth century.

CONTENTS.

COMPLETE INSTRUCTION

IN

REARING SILKWORMS.

SILKWORMS.

Silkworms come from the eggs of the silk-moth (*Bombyx mori*). The eggs are about the size of mustard seed. When first laid, they are yellow, afterward they change to a dark slate-color. As worms, they have five ages,—one as the chrysalis, and one as the miller; so that we may say truly, the silkworm has seven ages.

When the worms are first hatched from the eggs, they are about an eighth of an inch long, all covered with black hairs, that fall off in a few days. The head is black and shiny.

When the worms are nearly ready to come out of the shell, by the use of a magnifier the worm may be very plainly seen coiled round the outer edge of the shell. One black spot shows very conspicuously. That is the head of the insect. The eggs are slightly depressed in the center after the vitalized particles concentrate round the outer edge of the eggs to form the bodies of the worms. When the moment of perfect maturity

9

arrives, the worms burst a little hole in each shell, and crawl out head first. They immediately seek for food. The great cycle of silkworm life (i. e., from the egg to the egg again) is from thirty-six to forty-six days. When about four days old, they pass into a kind of sleep, called

Beginning of Second Age

End of Second Age

molt, in which condition they remain twenty-four hours, when they are said to molt,—that means, throwing off the entire old skin They first throw off the head-covering, and then crawl out of the body skin, which remains attached to the leaves or tray where they were when resting during the molt, or slumber. While in the first molt, worms look like little bits of rusty wire

As they come out of the comatose state, the body is a silvery gray, and the head a light

Beginning of Third Age

End of Third Age

brown. This is the second age. Very soon after molting they require food They continue to grow rapidly for five days more, and then again relapse into a comatose state and wake to the third age.

In about the same time the silkworm sleeps its third sleep, and awakes to the fourth age of its brief life, to eat more and grow faster. In this age the general formation of the worm is more easily studied. They require much more room, as well as food.

The next molt is the most critical period in silkworm life, and in countries where diseases rage, the silk-raisers are most anxious, as at this time they are sometimes liable to lose almost their entire crop through disease; for then, if any latent infectious disease has been lurking in them, it is sure to manifest itself.

In the fourth molt the worms are a very interesting study, as then they are large enough to permit of close observation of every movement, especially with the aid of a magnifier. When in the act of molting they become rigid. The head-covering becomes loose, and sometimes drops off before they are free from the old skin of the body; but it more often holds on by a single thread or bit of the shell until after the worms are entirely free. Sometimes it remains, hanging loosely, for a good while. Nature is very wonderful in all her works,—in nothing more than in the silk-worm. As the labor of molting goes on, the old skin is seen to be separate from the new, which has formed all over the body during their molt. Between the old and the new skin there is a

Beginning of Fourth Age.

watery fluid, provided so that the worms can more easily slide out of the old covering. This action is still further aided by the little horn that is always seen on the back, near the tail of the worm.

When the worms have ceased to eat before each molt, they fasten themselves to the place where

End of Fourth Age.

they are resting. This fastens the old skin so that it is held on the spot while the worm crawls out of its old house into a seemingly new life.

Skin of Worm.   Head-covering.

By lifting the old skin up, the entire outline of the worms may be traced, as the skin is stretched out while yet moist.

When the worms pass through the fourth molt, they are very soft and limp, and remain sometimes for hours without eating. They gradually gain appetite, and in a couple of days are well filled out and lively, have clear white or yellowish

Sixth Day of Fourth Molt.

skins, and for six or eight days are voracious eaters. Then they seem to lose appetite, and lie in one place on the trays, or else roam about in search of a place to spin the cocoons. Before they are absolutely ready to do this, all the waste matter or excrement is expelled from the body, and the worms, in consequence of this fact, are

Seventh Day of Fourth Molt.

less in size, and have assumed a semi-transparent appearance, and seem like little sacks of silken fluid.

During the life of the silkworm, it secretes from the mulberry leaf not only the soft, beautiful silk of the world, but also the necessary substance for the generating or reproducing its kind for succeeding generations.

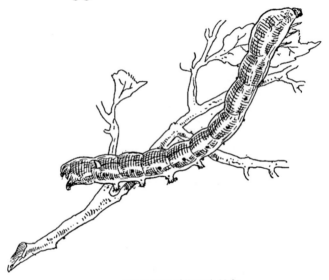

Ninth Day of Fourth Molt.

The worm secretes the silk in two membranous tubes, that fold and enfold in longitudinal layers nearly the whole length of the body. These tubes taper toward the upper end, and terminate in two little holes, called spinnerets, in the lower jaws. Through these holes the silk passes out of the worm, and is by it arranged layer upon layer all over the cocoon till all the silk substance is emitted from the tubes. This process is called

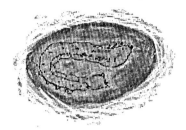

Worm Spinning the Cocoon.

spinning the cocoon, as shown above. If the worms are well cared for, and of good stock, at

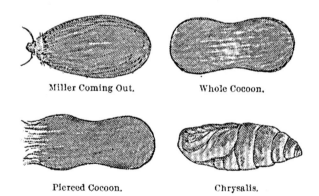

Miller Coming Out.   Whole Cocoon.

Pierced Cocoon.   Chrysalis.

the end of the fifth age they will measure $3\frac{1}{2}$ or 4 inches. They are elongated and cylindrical in form, and at this age measure $1\frac{3}{4}$ inches in circumference.

The head, which is almost circular, is covered with a thin shell. On either side of the head are four eyes, that stand out like little pearls.

The mouth is in the center of the head, and lies up and down, instead of across, as in most other insects and animals.

Near the eyes are two major feelers, which they use on all objects with which they come in contact. Nearer the mouth are two smaller feelers, used for similar purposes. Then come the two little holes called spinnerets, through which the silk comes from the silk-tubes as it passes up in very fine fibers to the cocoon.

The motion the worm makes with its head as it spins the cocoon, twists the two fine filaments into one as each double circle is laid on over and over again and again without any variation or tangling, provided the worms have been properly cared for and left undisturbed in a warm atmosphere during the time of spinning the cocoons.

The use of a magnifier will show that the bodies of worms in the fourth and fifth ages are covered over with a kind of bristle resembling pig's bristles, though not nearly so numerous as on the swine.

The silkworm has sixteen paws. The first

three pair are seen on the thorax, or chest, of the insect. They are called the *true*, or permanent, legs, because they remain in the miller state; while the other five pair, seen on either side of the abdomen, disappear as the worm becomes the miller. These last-named paws are thicker than the others, and are heavily covered with down, or fine hairs. They serve the worm to hold on to the branches, as well as to enable it to walk straight forward without bending the body, as the measuring-worm does when it moves. The two lower of these paws are situated on the sides of the extreme end of the worm, and serve a very good purpose in holding on with fast grip to any object on which it climbs.

The entire body of the worm is divided into twelve rings. The first three surround the thorax, or chest, and are not so very distinctly marked as the other nine, which are on the lower portion of the body. The last pair are on either side of the fan-shaped termination of the abdomen, above and between which is the anus. On the upper side of the eighth ring is a small, sharp, horn-like organ. This serves as a movable lever when the worm is molting, as it moves back and forth with the movement of the worm as it crawls out of the old skin, which it lifts up, and thus keeps it from clinging to the new skin.

Right in the center of the back, under the skin, is to be seen a straight, thread-like organ, which always pulsates regularly when the worm is in a healthy condition This seems to contain the food in the first process of digestion. Below this organ, on either side, and closer to the feet, are nine small spots or holes surrounded by short black hairs. These are the breathing apertures of the worm, as it does not, like most insects and animals, breathe through the nostrils or mouth.

If the worm be examined with a powerful lens when nearly ready to spin, it may be seen that from these little holes small, black thread-like organs ramify over the inside surface of the skin. These may also be seen if the worm be dissected, and the skin freed from its contents. These will remain and be very clearly seen, radiating in all directions from the center. The silkworm has five senses; viz., hearing, seeing, smelling, tasting, and feeling. Of these, the senses of smell and taste are the keenest. However young a silkworm may be, it will at once crawl in the direction of a fresh mulberry leaf and begin to eat. They are very careful not to taste or eat anything that will disagree with them, unless driven by starvation. The silkworm is a cold-blooded insect and so it is that it always maintains the temperature of the atmosphere in which it is reared.

SEX OF THE SILKWORM.

Concerning the sex of the silkworm, — how to detect it in the different stages of its changeful life, etc., it is queried which makes the most and the best silk, etc.; but the question is as yet an open one, waiting for some as yet unknown "savant" to arise and settle the whole matter.

I will here offer my theory, searched out within the past few years, and submitted for just what it is worth. It is based on the harmonies of nature, and is as follows: —

The sex is not determined by the manner of feeding, either abundantly or otherwise. It is not in the ovum of the female; but it is in the semen of the male, the same as it is in all animal nature. In speaking of creation, the Bible says, "Male and female created he them." This was said of the highest type of animal life, and of course it embraced all the lesser types, however infinitesimal they may appear to us.

So far as science has yet discovered, in all perfect males there are two sacs, which contain the seminal fluid, or vitalizing principle. One of these contains the male and the other the female element. These life-germs are injected into the ovum, or egg, which is lodged in the womb of the female insect, or animal. In the silkworm this organ differs very much from larger types of animal life. In the silk-miller it consists of long, slender membranous tubes, folding and enfolding longitudinally in the body of the female miller. In dissecting the insects, these tubes may be stretched out so that the eggs appear like strings of the smallest pearls inside the tubes.

When the male and female millers are coupled, the vitalizing substance passes up these tubes and fertilizes the eggs. In the body of the female miller there is a strong ligament passing down the body to the extreme end. When she deposits her eggs, this ligament extends into sight, and on either side appears an egg, which she carefully deposits, and attaches to the material on which she lays; then she in like manner deposits from the other side, and so on, till all her store of eggs has been expelled from the body. Here I hold that sex is distinctly and separately deposited, having been previously determined in the body of the male. There must be a beginning of the sex, and when once begun, it *never* can be changed by human action or invention.

It is quite possible that a more careful application of the X rays may give more light on this subject.

FEEDING SILKWORMS.

When the worm has sufficiently developed in the shell, it makes a hole in the side and comes out, usually head first. At first it is all covered with black hairs, or fine feathers, similar to those which in after life appear all over the body and wings of the miller. These hairs fall off in a few days. At first the worm is about an eighth of an inch long.

If the eggs are kept in cold-storage, they should be brought by degrees from a temperature of 40° F., first to 50°, then 60°, then 70°, at which temperature they should be kept night and day till the worms have spun their cocoons They should never be placed either in the draft or sunshine. Within from seven to twenty days from the time of taking the eggs from cold-storage they will begin to hatch out of the shells.

If the eggs were all right when put in, ninety-five per cent, at least, will come out. A very slight clicking noise will be heard from the trays on which the eggs are spread out. This is caused by the bursting of the shells, and soon multitudes of worms will be seen crawling among the eggs and empty shells. The worms hatch out in the morning.

Within the first hour after they begin to appear, take a piece of mosquito-netting already prepared, and spread it over the worms. Have ready some young mulberry leaves cut as fine as cut tobacco (not chopped like salad), and sprinkle the leaves evenly over the worms. If they are very numerous and come up quickly, take off that piece of netting soon and place it on a clean tray, and put on another piece of netting as at the first, and also sprinkle with the cut leaves On the first tray place a card with the words, " First hatch, May 10, 1902," or whatever the date may happen to be Be sure that this card is kept with the first hatch throughout all the changes and molts. In an hour or so, remove the second piece of netting, and mark it as " Second hatch," with date as before directed, and so on, in like manner, for three days, or until the eggs have all hatched.

Never lose the dates, or in any way mix the trays of worms. Then they will all molt at the same time, and will all be ready to spin at the same time.

In about two or three hours after the first feed, feed again, and so on for four days, and as late as ten or eleven o'clock at night, and by five every morning. They will begin to lose their appetite on the third or fourth day, and will soon refuse to eat, and fall into a kind of slumber, which is called the first molt. While in this state they look like little bits of rusty wire. On the morning of the fourth or fifth day may be seen a slight, quick motion among the little worms, as they shake off their old head-coverings, and crawl out of their little skins, and set out on a search for food. This should be given them as at the first, by spreading frésh netting over the trays and sprinkling fresh-cut leaves over them. The worms have now changed appearance. The head is a light brownish color, the body a light silver-gray. They eat heartily, and should be fully gratified with fresh, wholesome leaves, either cut in strips as wide as they are long, or else the whole leaves on the branchlets. When leaves are cut, they should be rolled up as hard as can be, in rolls an inch in diameter. Hold them tight with the left hand, and cut down across through the middle. Then put both halves together, and slice down the leaves till the roll is all cut. Toss them up with the hand, and then they will sprinkle lightly wherever you need them.

During this age the worms measure from one half to three quarters of an inch. In four or five days they lose appetite, and again fall into a stupor or molt. In this they remain as at the first, and awake to eat and grow, and grow and eat, continuously. When they awake from this the second molt, unless there be very coarse netting or perforated paper, it is best to feed by putting on, very carefully, small branches. Care must be taken not to let the twigs rest on the little worms so as to crush them. Let each worm have about the square of itself on the tray.

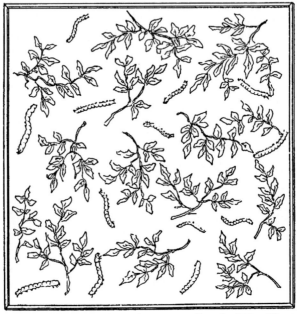

Tray with leaves spread over the worms as they should be   There is room for many more than appear in the cut.

When the worms are fed with cut leaves, the trays should be emptied of all refuse leaves, and well aired every day or every other day, if the weather be very dry and clear. The waste matter, if left, is very apt to sour, and such a condition will surely affect the worms unfavorably. Too much care cannot be given to cleanliness in every department of the cocoonery.

The second molt brings the worms to the third age. They undergo the same period of inactivity. It is more noticeable how soft and limp they are after the change, but they very soon "fill up," and during this age they measure from 1 to $1\frac{1}{4}$ inches in length. Each successive molt seems to affect the worms more and more seriously, and they are more slow in recovering from the effect of what, in some countries, is called their sicknesses. Their long fast, and the extra exertion of casting their skins, is a severe drain on their vitality, which it requires a little time to recover.

The third molt comes on in five or six days more. In this the fourth age they seem to grow more rapidly than before. They eat very freely, and, too, of more mature leaves. In this age they should be fed very freely. The branches, fresh and clean, should be laid on every three or four hours. Indeed, they should never be left without fresh food all day. A feed at ten or eleven o'clock at night, and another between mid-

night and three, A. M., will be found of great use
in the increase of both the quantity and quality
of silk, as well as giving ability to the worms to
complete their work in a shorter time, than if left
to roam over empty branches, looking in vain
for food. In this age the worms grow to 1½ to 2
inches, and hence many more trays will have to
be provided, as it is not best at any time to crowd
worms on the trays. The fourth and last molt is
the most critical in silkworm life. In silk countries, where diseases are prevalent, there is most
anxiety felt, as then most ailments are manifested,
and often a large part of the silk crop is lost
through disease. Great care should be taken to
give an abundance of fresh air, fresh food, and
plenty of room, both on the trays and in the
racks. At first, and for a few days, they seem
soft and limp, but soon they eat voraciously and
grow strong, and seem as plump as little sausages.
They seem to make a *business* of eating, and attend strictly to it. In this age, especially, they
never should be left an hour without fresh food.

During the last two days of the fifth age they
will not eat so much, and gradually lose all desire
for food, and wander over the trays, looking for
places to spin their cocoons. Sometimes they will
settle on one spot of the tray and wait till all the
refuse matter passes from their bodies, and then
they look for a place to deposit their load of silk.

Wherever silkworms locate to spin, whether on the tray, under the dry leaves, in a canopy in branches (or little round coops, where they may be placed for closer inspection), they *always* throw out silk threads or strands to sustain themselves while spinning their cocoons. .

They fix these strands back and forth to the adjacent object. When they feel themselves secure, they proceed to draw the outlines of the cocoons, and then pass all round the cocoons, putting on a fresh layer each time, till their store of silk-fluid is all exhausted. Every thread of silk is put on in a double circle, and for this reason it never tangles in being taken off. A perfect cocoon is the same thickness all round.

The silk comes out through two little holes called spinnerets, where, as before stated, the silk tubes or ducts terminate. The motion that the worms make with their heads in the act of putting the silk on the cocoons twists these two threads into one.

If worms are properly cared for, they will spin their cocoons in two or three days. In feeding branches during the last three ages of the worms, it is well to lay the branches lengthwise and then crosswise, so as to form a kind of latticework of the branches. The worms crawl over these branches and eat the leaves directly from them. This mode of feeding allows a much better circulation of air, and prevents the worms from crowding on one another. When fed solid leaves, they are very apt to mat down, and then become heated and emit an unsavory odor, which never should be allowed in the cocoonery.

If the air of the room be very pure and dry, and the lower branches become dry, it is not necessary to remove the worms to clean trays every day, but if the refuse and the portions of leaves not eaten seem moist and likely to mold or sour, they should be changed to fresh trays by lifting the branches, the upper layers with the worms on them. Set them on fresh trays, and put the used trays out to air, and let them be perfectly dried before using again. It is many times best, as it saves much time and labor to take out the trays from the racks. Spread a cloth (such as is used to cover the leaves to keep the moisture in) on the floor, take one tray at a time, lay one side on the cloth, and hold the other at an angle of about fifty degrees. Hold the frame with your left hand, and with the right hand gently lift up the branches and shake them so as to shake also the tray. In this way all the dirt and litter will roll down, and you can put the trays back in place and feed the worms. When there are two persons in the cocoonery, this work can be done very much more quickly.

ARRANGEMENTS FOR SPINNING.

When the worms find in themselves that they have extracted from their food and stored away in their silk cells or ducts all the silk they can retain, they begin to look for a place to spin. Something in their nature prompts them to look up, and if no proper place be provided, they will even crawl up to the ceiling, and form their cocoons by attaching them to the ceiling and the wall

A great many ways have been tried by those who have from time to time engaged in the silk business in this country. Some have tried branches laid transversely all over the trays, mixing with the branches coarse straw, or excelsior, or paper torn in strips. Others put the branches all round the trays where they are feeding, and hope they will take to the branches when they get ready to spin. Others make arches of branches over the spinning-trays, and let the worms mount up into the arches when they get ready. This is a very good way, but very troublesome, and calls for a constant renewal of the branches, as they cannot very readily be cleaned Others, again, make frames something like the feeding-trays, only the frames are deeper, by turning the slats the opposite way. They are covered with burlap, and over the frames mosquito-netting is drawn tightly, and tacked all round. Then there are a few holes cut, about one by one half-inch, in the netting. When the worms are all ready to spin, they are taken up gently and dropped into these holes, and a piece of pasteboard laid over the holes to keep them from getting away They will wander about for a while, but being unable to get out, they will finally settle down and spin. It is wise to put in these frames something to keep the netting from sagging down; also put in some wads of crinkled paper,—newspaper will do, if you have nothing better. Worms always want something near-by to cling to as they throw out their supporting strands of silk.

Another mode is to suspend branches from the tray above. Fix them so as to just touch the tray on which the worms are. Some of them will mount, but they are liable to wander about.

Yet another style is to take a tray such as the worms feed on, and pile it up about a foot high with little branches and pieces of crinkled paper. Let them be loosely put on. Then set this tray between two trays that are ready to spin, and the worms will crawl up on either side. The tray fixed for spinning will accommodate both the other trays, as there will be several tiers among the branches.

All these different methods have their advantages and disadvantages

The greatest objection to them all is, that the worms are at liberty to roam where they will, and they *will* wander about till they find suitable places in which to spin their cocoons. Besides, wherever branches are used, they have to be renewed almost every time they are used. This is a great trouble, as it is hard to find suitable branches in many places in California. Another thing is, the branches have to be very clean, else they will give the cocoons a soiled and objectionable appearance, which detracts from their market value.

Having proved all the above arrangements for worms to spin in to be unsatisfactory, during the summer of 1901 I designed and had made what I call a canopy. This I believe to be, all points considered, the best and most economical of anything yet presented to the public in this line of the silk industry. The special points of advantage are as follows: —

1 When once made, these canopies will last a lifetime.

2. They can always be kept clean.

3. When not in use, they can be stored away

in comparatively small space; and they are always ready for use.

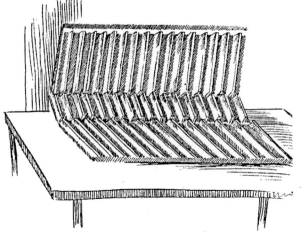

No. 1 Canopy open on a table.

No. 2 Canopy closed on the tray, showing cocoons in the canopy and mulberry leaves on the table.

4. The cocoons in them are always clean.

5. The worms are above all *débris*, which, when dry, often hurts their tender little bodies. It may all be removed when all the worms have mounted, and the trays brushed out without disturbing the worms.

6. The worms, being elevated, can get plenty of fresh air, which is an essential to them while spinning.

7. The cocoons, when ready, are taken from the canopies in far less time than from any of the arrangements before mentioned. When the cocoons are ready to be taken out, take the piece of cloth from the gable end of the canopy and lift it from the tray, lay it on a table or stretcher opened out as it was before being put on the tray, then pass the hand up and down through each compartment, taking the cocoons out by the handful If there be much floss left on the slats, take a damp cloth or brush and pass it up and down, and it will readily adhere and come off, leaving the canopy all clean. Place on the tray, and it is ready to be again used.

DESCRIPTION OF CANOPY.

2 slats 30 inches long, 1 x $\frac{1}{2}$ inch wide.

4 slats 30 inches long, 1 x $\frac{1}{4}$ inch wide.

36 slats 17 inches long, 1 x $\frac{1}{4}$ inch wide.

18 slats 10 inches long, 1 x $\frac{1}{4}$ inch wide.

The two 30-inch slats are the two bottom-stays of the canopy, into which are jointed the 36 slats 17 inches long, 18 into each slat. The upper ends are jointed into two of the other 30-inch slats. This completes the two sides Into the other two 30-inch slats are jointed the eighteen 10-inch slats, which forms the top of the canopy. The two upper edges of the sides are placed by the two outer edges of the top piece, and fastened together by two pairs of small hinges. Strips of strong cloth may be glued on, instead of hinges.

Now take a piece of unbleached muslin, a few inches longer than the canopy when stretched out. Spread it all over smoothly. Have four very thin strips ($\frac{1}{4}$-inch will do), 30 inches long, and tack them on the slats into which the 17-inch upright strips are jointed, and the 10-inch strips for the top. Tack down the strips with small brads, having first very carefully stretched the cloth straight and tight. These strips will hold the cloth firmly on top of the canopy. Turn it upside down on the table and fasten all the outer edges of the cloth onto the outer edges of the frame with paste made of flour and water boiled. Apply with a brush or the hand. Have a feeding-tray ready by driving two-inch nails in each side six inches from the ends and one half-inch from the edges.

Lift up the canopy from the table and let it come together as near as the top piece will admit it. Set it on the tray, inside the nails which are designed to keep it in place. Then take a piece of the same kind of cloth as the cover, and stretch it over one end, fastening it on with pins. Put three or four in the lower end, on the tray, and the others on the canopy. The lower pins need not often be removed When the paste is dry, the canopy is ready to be placed over a tray of worms that are all ready to spin. Have the tray ready with the nails in before you put the worms on. Take out the lower pins and lay the canopy over the worms. Again pin down the end piece, and you will soon see them mounting up the narrow streets and all over the top, and in due time every spot will have a clean, beautiful cocoon.

It is always best to put in a few branches under the canopy at first, and even several times, if the worms are slow in going up to spin.

These canopies seem to be very troublesome affairs at first; but when it is remembered how long they last and how much better the work is done in them, the balance is largely in their favor.

COCOONS—HOW TO CARE FOR THEM.

The cocoons out of which the millers have come are called pierced cocoons. They have a commercial value only equal to that of waste silk When the millers come out, they leave behind them in the cocoons both the skins of the worms in which they existed while spinning the cocoons, and also the shells of the chrysalis into which they passed from the worm state, and again into the miller, which is the last, or seventh, age of silkworm life.

Where pierced cocoons are used, these animal substances are dissolved by chemicals, and then the silk is cleansed before it is carded and spun for manufacturing

The cocoons that are not pierced should be steamed within six or seven days after the worms mounted to spin If working on a small scale, have a boiler of water at the boiling-point before you put the cocoons to steam, as it kills them much quicker. Put them into a tray, as hereafter described, not more than three or four inches deep. Cover them over with a clean cloth, and then with several folds of newspaper, so as to retain in with the cocoons every particle of steam. Let none be scattered outside the rim of the boiler. Let them steam twenty minutes or half an hour. Remove the papers; lift off the tray from the boiler and deftly turn it upside down on another tray; let the steam pass off, and in a short time the cocoons will have sufficiently hardened for you to separate them and spread them out to dry. In a day or two, they had better be put in cotton bags, each bag about three quarters full. Hang up the bags in an airv place to dry, and toss them up in the bags every day. This can be done without untying the bags.

If working on a large scale in a cocoonery, the better way would be to have a fruit-dryer, and heat the dryer hot enough to kill the chrysalis, and afterwards keep it hot enough to thoroughly dry the cocoons.

Great care is necessary in the caring for as well as in the drying of cocoons. In order to keep them from molding, every particle of moisture must be absorbed. They must be *thoroughly desiccated.* Insects and mice are very fond of the chrysalis, and will destroy the cocoons to get at them.

Cocoons are designated by their color, as well as by the race of worms from which they come. The most noted and best varieties now used in Europe are the small yellow Italian, the large yellow French, the white Japanese, and the Turkish white.

There are two principal varieties used in Japan,
—the deep yellow and the pure white, the latter
. said to produce the finest silk in the world.

Green cocoons are not now held in high esteem
by any nation. The silk is very soft, but not as
strong as either the white or yellow.

GREEN AND DRY COCOONS

Green or fresh cocoons are those that are just
spun, as also up to the time when they are perfectly dry. They should never be put away or
packed in close vessels, or even in sacks, because
they are very apt to mold. The sacks when
half full may be shaken up every day, and in
that way the cocoons may be dried. If a filature
is near-by, it is better to dispose of green cocoons,
than to spend the time drying them.

It will require 150 to 600 green cocoons to
weigh one pound   It requires three to three and
a half times as many dry cocoons to give the
same weight   The price of dry cocoons is as
much greater as the weight is less.

QUANTITY OF SILK ON COCOONS.

The best breed of cocoons, under the most careful management, will yield eighteen hundred
yards of silk.   As yet, we have none of this breed
in the United States   Our good stock will yield

one thousand to fifteen hundred yards, while
those insignificant, illy cared for, papery cocoons,
raised merely for pastime or pleasure, will scarce
give off two hundred yards. This shows the folly
of attempting to do work the wrong way. It
gives a false impression of the real value of the
silk business.

The relative value of cocoons is determined by
color, sinew, evenness of thread, and freedom
from gum. The white Japan are said to have
less gum than any other breed we have here.
The silk from yellow or green cocoons can never
be bleached as white as the silk from the pure
white. Neither will the silk from colored cocoons
take the most delicate shades of dye. This is
one of the reasons why the pure white cocoons
are in greater demand than the colored.

Double cocoons have, as a rule, very strong
silk, but as they cannot be reeled because the two
worms, working together, tangle the silk on the
cocoons, they are valueless for reeling, and therefore their value is only that of waste silk.

In France, the price of cocoons ranges, for green
cocoons, from 30 to 35 cents; for dry cocoons,
from 80 cents to $1.50 per pound. The same
prices should be paid in the United States, or
even more.

Twelve hundred good cocoons with the insect
entirely removed will weigh one pound.

COCOONS FOR BREEDING.

When the cocoons are taken from the branches, trays, or canopies where they were spun, select the best,—i. e., the most regular in shape and the most evenly spun. Have shallow boxes about two inches deep all ready, with soft paper in the bottoms, and take alternately a large plump cocoon and a long slender one, and lay them one tier deep in the boxes. Handle them very gently, and lay the boxes away in the hatching-room, or on trays, where they will not be disturbed. Do not let them be in the draft or sunshine at any time. Keep the temperature up to 70° all the time of incubation. In eight or ten days from the selecting of the cocoons, early in the morning the millers will begin to emerge from their silken homes.

MILLERS—HOW TO CARE FOR THEM.

When the millers make their appearance from
the cocoons, at first they are wet all over. The
head first appears, and they gradually work
themselves out till the entire body is free from
its cage. Their general appearance is as if they
had risen from a bath.

The male millers, as soon as they are out, at
once go on a search for their mates. They cease-
lessly flutter their wings as they go from one to
another, till they at last find a female with which
they couple. Let all that will, couple and remain
coupled for six hours. If there come out more
of one sex than the other, the odd ones should be
removed to another box till the next day, when,
perhaps, the balance will be made even, and all
will eventually be mated. Sometimes the millers
will separate before the end of six hours. When
this occurs, it is well to remove the male from
the box and put another in his place, or else put
the female in the box with the surplus males. In
a very short time she will couple with a fresh
male. Then lift them gently by the wings of the
female and place them in the mating-box with
the others.

When the time is up to separate the millers,

Male Miller.

have shallow boxes ready, and place smoothly in the bottom of each box one or more sheets of blank newspaper (which can be bought at stationers at ten cents a pound). On both sides

Miller and Eggs.

should be written the color of the cocoon from which the millers came, the day of the month, and the year. It is well, also, to put strips of paper round the sides of the boxes, as the millers at times lay on the sides of the boxes Cover the boxes and lay them aside in a quiet, dark room for forty-eight hours. Then the millers may be thrown away, if not wanted to be preserved for fancy-work or demonstration when preserved and mounted.

When the business is carried on on a large scale, instead of boxes a room is so arranged by dividing it into compartments having partitions six or eight inches high, running the entire length of the room. These aisles should be about twenty-eight inches wide, with an aisle about twelve inches between This is to allow the attendant to care for the millers

When the millers are separated and placed in boxes or aisles to lay, each miller should be allowed the square of itself, so that there be no crowding If at the appointed time the millers have not all separated, take hold of the female miller by both wings with the left hand, and the male with the right hand, and with the third finger press lightly on the abdomen of the male This act will make it loosen its hold. Many millers lay their eggs in a few hours after being put away. The best eggs are laid *en masse,* or in semicircles. Eggs that are laid scattering about are, as a rule, not worth saving. They never should be laid in heaps.

When taken from the boxes, the papers should be hung on files from the wall, so they will not press one on the other.

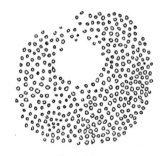

Best Eggs.

Silkworm eggs are about the size of mustard seed, not orange-shape, but depressed on both upper and under side. When first laid they are yellow, and, viewed with a magnifier, they seem full of liquid of the same hue. They may be considered as annuals, bivoltines, and polyvoltines. Annuals hatch once a year; bivoltines, twice; and polyvoltines, three, four, or more times, according to their good or careless feeding or care.

In two or three days after laying. those that are seen to begin to change color will not hatch out very soon. In a few more days they will have become quite a dark slate-color, and a magnifiying-glass will show that each egg is full of a liquid in which is floating very fine spots or particles, some larger than others. These little spots are the vitalized particles, that in due time collect round the outer edge of the shell, condense, and produce the little worm, which, as soon as nature has completed her work inside the shell, comes to the outside world through a hole in the side of the shell. As the work of developing the worm progresses, the center of the shell becomes depressed, and the edge elevated as the growth of the worm inside presses it up.

The polyvoltines, or those eggs that will hatch out within ten days to three weeks, do not change to darker color, as the others, but, instead, there may be seen in them, at the end of the fourth or fifth day, a sort of filmy substance all through the shell. Gradually this condenses toward the outer edge, and then is seen, apparently, the outline of the worm, though so filmy and light as to be almost invisible. In a few more days the eggs are a bright lavender or slate color, and the entire form of the worm may be distinctly seen. Then very soon the little worm will hatch out and look for its natural food, mulberry leaves.

Scientific experiments have proved that silkworm eggs may be so managed that with the aid of cold-storage (below 40° F.) they may be kept more than a year, and taken out whenever the food and accommodations for them are all ready.

Eggs must be put into cold-storage while yet the vital particles are seen floating separately in the fluid contained in the shell. If they are put into storage *after* these particles begin to concentrate round the outer edge of the egg forming the outline of the worm, it is too late, and the worm is at once chilled, and perishes.

Eggs should be packed in layers of wadding to keep the eggs from pressing too heavily on each other. They should be put in a tin or sheet-iron or even wooden box, and covered closely, having a layer of wadding on the top, inside the cover. The box containing the eggs should be placed in another box about three inches larger all round. The space between the two boxes should be filled with some woolen material to reject the dampness if the storage be in a moist place. When the box is opened to take out eggs for hatching, it should *never* be removed to a warmer room. The eggs should be taken out as quickly as possible and the box again closed up. By observing the foregoing instruction, the fact of producing silkworms is completely under human control, and can be done at *any time* and at all seasons of the year.

COCOONERY.

A cocoonery should always be built on a slight elevation of ground, so that in time of rain the water will not settle round the building. All things considered, a good wooden building is quite good enough for California. The ends of the building should be to the east and west, so that the sun will not strike with fullest force in hot summer weather.

It is better to have a cocoonery rest on posts two or three feet from the ground, to give free circulation, as also to keep off all kinds of insects. The posts should be daubed with tar or some other substance to prevent insects from climbing into the building.

SIZE AND STYLE OF COCOONERY.

To accommodate the product of three ounces of silk-eggs (i. e., 120,000 worms) will require a building forty by fifty feet, twelve feet between floor and ceiling. The roof should be as sloping as the width of the building will admit. The floor should be double, because, standing upon posts, it will thus maintain a more even temperature. The walls and ceiling should be lined with wood. Smooth or planed boards are best, as they will not retain dust. There should be three ventilators, twelve by twelve inches, in the ceiling, one over each aisle. These should be of fine wire, to keep out insects, and should be so fixed that a board may fall over them when necessary to keep off the draft. There should also be two ventilators in the roof, with wire screens to use at will, and yet so arranged as to keep out both rain and fog.

It is advisable to have a trap-door in some part of the ceiling, so that one can get up in the garret if necessary. There should be three windows on each side of the building, at equal distance from the ends and from each other. Also, two windows in each end, one on either side of the vestibule, which should be in the center. This should be about five by six feet, with an outside and inside door. The upper half of each door should be glass. The utility of these vestibules is to keep off sudden gusts of air from the worms when the doors are opened.

Have wire screens from top to bottom of all the windows, which should open both above and below. There should also be either inside slat-shutters, or paper blinds, to adjust the light.

A single board partition should divide the building into two rooms. The smaller on the east end, fifteen by forty feet; the larger, thirty-five by forty feet. The large room may have a five-foot aisle all across each end, and four double racks, each one five feet wide and twenty-five feet long. There should be three aisles, each three feet wide, between the double racks. These spaces leave room to draw out the trays from the racks when the worms are being attended to.

There is a space of five and a half feet on either side of the racks between them and the wall. In this space two single racks may be placed on either side of the room, leaving the opposite diagonal corners for two tables, which will be found necessary for various kinds of work. The single racks should be two and a half feet deep and six feet long, so they will take in but three trays across, instead of four. They should be seven feet high, the same as the others.

SMALL ROOM.

This room should have a door in the center of the partition dividing it from the large room. There should be a transom over the door. From the southeast end of the room, there should be partitioned off a room ten by fifteen feet. The partition need be but seven feet high. On the northeast end have a dark closet, fifteen feet against the inner wall and seven feet on the outside wall. This may be seven feet high, and the top covered with lattice-work, so that when necessary it can be made perfectly dark by spreading cloth or papers over the lattice. Let the door be half glass. Have shelves about two feet deep all round, except at the door, and all the way up and down, within a foot of the floor. These should be of light lumber. This will serve as a laying-room for millers, also for storing eggs till they are put in cold-storage, and for various other purposes.

The other small room will be required for leaves, to store, so as to have them always ready. In this room there should be a hydrant and a tank, or bath-tub, in which to wash the leaves when they happen to be dusty. Great care must be taken not to let dampness rest, so as to vitiate the air.

In the other part of the small room have a single rack like those in the large room. Instead of trays, have shelves, as in the dark closet. A few chairs or camp-stools will be required at times in both rooms.

Everything connected with the cocoonery must be kept as clean and free from all odors as it is possible. The floors had better be oiled or painted, so that they will dry quickly when mopped. They never should be allowed to get very dusty, as dust is not wholesome for the silkworms.

Unless hot-air pipes can be provided, oil-stoves will do for heating, but they must be a kind that will not give off any odor. When the air seems too dry, a vessel of water should be placed on the stove.

FURNITURE OF COCOONERY.

The cocoonery should be fumigated every week by burning eucalyptus leaves. All the ventilators should be opened in three minutes to let the smoke escape. This process purifies the atmosphere.

Have four double racks five feet deep and twenty-five feet long. These are for the large room. An aisle three feet wide should pass through the center of the room, between the two middle racks. Another aisle the same width should separate each of the other double racks. In these aisles the stretchers may be placed to attend to the worms.

In the wider spaces at either side of the room, two single racks can be placed between the windows, also two common tables, that will often be needed. Six or eight stretchers will be found useful for many purposes, especially to lay trays on when working with the worms or millers.

*Lumber Required for Racks and Trays for the
Large Room*

One single rack will require —

28 feet of scantling, 3 x 3 inches. This is for four posts.

70 feet for ten upright stays, 1 x 2 inches.

35 feet, 2 x 3 inches, for the sides and ends of the top of the rack.

360 feet of slats, 1 x $\frac{1}{2}$ inch.

460 feet of lathing for 36 trays.

In computing for the lumber, get enough for four double racks and four single ones for the large room, and one for the small room, and enough lathing and burlap for 720 trays, 24 x 30 inches, and twelve one half as large, to be covered with white goods, same as used to cover the canopies Also, get shelving for closet of small room and rack-shelves.

To Put the Rack Together

Fasten the four posts to the two top pieces which are 12$\frac{1}{2}$ feet long, also the ten stays a little more than 24 inches apart. Then put the two sides of the rack together by fastening the end pieces to the sides Next fasten in the slides 14 inches apart This will leave space enough between the trays, at least till the last age. It may be that the branches are too large then. If so, take out every alternate tray.

TRAYS.

Make the trays 24 inches wide and 30 inches long, with two slats across, to keep them from sagging. Cover with a medium quality of burlap Draw it very tightly over the tray and fasten with tacks on the sides, so that it will slide in and out smoothly. In putting the racks together, there must be room enough left for the trays to slip in and out readily, as the worms must never be shaken up or jerked about more than is absolutely necessary. It will be found that the posts and uprights, when held together by so many slats, make the racks quite strong enough.

Some prefer larger trays, and would have the trays doubled. But, all things considered, I prefer the size indicated, for many reasons They are more easily handled at all times, and especially when the worms are in the two last ages. When they are ready to spin, these trays just fit the canopies, and when in the canopies they have more room, or, rather, there are not so many under one cover. When spinning, the worms should have plenty of fresh air. The material necessary for the canopies is described under the heading, "Arrangements for Spinning."

Two canopies will afford room enough for three

trays of worms to spin, or even four, provided the trays are not very full. If the worms are large and fine, as they always ought to be, 100 to 125 is quite enough for a tray.

What I have termed "stretchers" are made something like bamboo music-racks or holders. Slats one by one half inch, and three feet long, are crossed for the legs. A round piece about three quarters of an inch in diameter and three feet long holds the cross-pieces together in the center. Two pieces at the top of the legs, the same length as the round center-piece, hold the sides or frame firmly. In these there should be holes one quarter inch, one in each cross-piece, six inches from the end. These will hold cords stretched from one to the other. Leave the cords long enough so that the stretcher can be adjusted high or low, as is required. These will hold canopies at any time after the worms have mounted to spin, if the racks be over-crowded.

TO PRESERVE SILKWORMS.

In this advanced age, it is quite desirable to have cases of preserved silkworms, as well as other insects, for exhibition and demonstration in schools and colleges. As a rule, this art is neither known nor practiced by silk-culturists. It seems too small an item of business to claim their attention from the greater and more pleasing work pertaining to the insect menagerie. However, this work may be done by any person whose taste and ambition run on scientific lines. I will therefore give a formula, which, if strictly followed, will insure success in this branch of science.

Get a bottle of hydroformalin at the druggist's. Have a two-quart bottle of distilled rain-water. Take ninety-six per cent of water and four per cent of the formalin. Let it be thoroughly mixed. Then take five pint or quart fruit-jars, according to the number of worms you desire to handle. Have the jars half or two-thirds full of the medicated water and drop the worms in, each age in a separate jar. The chrysalis may be put with worms of the fifth age. They will not suffer long. Whenever the water becomes discolored, pour off, and put in fresh liquid from the large bottle.

When it remains perfectly clear, the worms are preserved. This will require several days.

After the worms are dead, and before they get hard and stiff, they should be carefully taken out with nippers onto a glass slab or plate and straightened out, and it is best then to inflate with a hypodermic syringe, using some of the same fluid the worms are in. This process will enlarge the worms, as well as harden the internal organs. The syringe may be inserted in the anus, but great care must be taken not to puncture the internal organs. After this is done, they should be at once put back into the fluid

ARRANGEMENT FOR A CASE.

To prepare worms for a case for exhibition, have ready as many sets of bottles (five constitutes a full set) as you require. The bottles should be such as are used by naturalists, — i. e., without necks. The largest should be $4\frac{1}{2}$ inches long, the others gradually receding in length to the smallest, $1\frac{3}{4}$ inches. The corks must always be the best, and not more than a half-inch deep. A very appropriate finish for the cork is made by splitting cocoons in several layers. Then cut circles just the size of the corks, and glue them onto the corks. Put one worm of the fifth age in the largest bottle, and one of the fourth age in

the next-sized. Then in the next-sized bottle put
two of the third age, and in the two next sizes
put several of the first and second ages. Put two
chrysalises in one of the large bottles. There
should be ready a neat wooden box lined and
padded on the bottom. Any kind of nice goods,
not woolen, will answer. The bottles should be
arranged from left to right, beginning with the
first age and ending with the chrysalis. They
should be fastened to the bottom of the box, either
with glue or some other fastening.

TO DISSECT WORMS.

Take three worms in the fifth age, — one about
the middle of the age, one two days from spinning, and one all ready to spin. Drop them into
a pint jar of the same liquid as for the other
worms. Let them remain a few hours or all
night. Take out one at a time onto a glass slab
or plate, using the nippers. Lay the worm on
its back. Take sharp-pointed scissors, and cut
the worm open on the under side, the entire
length of the body, taking great care not to
pierce any of the internal organs. Have a shallow dish about two inches deep filled with pure
distilled water. Plunge the worm into this dish,
and float out the entire contents of the body into
the water (you may have to use the nippers, but

very gently), and you will then see the silk-ducts in longitudinal folds on either side of the worm. Be very careful not to break away the upper ends of the tubes from the spinnerets in the head of the worm, where they terminate. The middle of the duct is about one eighth of an inch in diameter, and tapers down at both ends till it is as fine as a thread of fine silk. The upper ends terminate in the spinnerets, and the lower ends pass over the entire inner surface of the body in folds and coils, while they imbibe the silk-fluid as it is distilled from the mulberry leaves by the action of nature's unerring machine, — the body of the silkworm.

On either side are seen those same eight little round black spots that are seen on the outside, and which serve as breathing-pores. From each of these radiate fine black thread-like tubes all over the side for some distance from the center spot. These carry the air to the body, and keep it in constant circulation, vitalizing or vitiating the whole system of the worm as the air is pure or impure in which the worm rests while doing its important work.

If the worm dissected be within two days of spinning, the long straight duct that, during life, may be seen passing up and down the whole length of the body, on the back, may now be

seen more plainly as a long narrow duct filled
with food in process of digestion.

If the worm is ready to spin, this duct will be
empty, and appear the same color as the other
parts of the body of the worm.

The youngest of the three worms dissected in
the same way will show a less proportion of silk
in the ducts and a greater proportion of food in
the body. There will be found adhering to the
inside of the skin a seemingly fatty substance,
according to the breed of worm and the quantity
and quality of food administered. This will be
more or less in quantity. In this substance of
the worm the fine ramifications of the silk-ducts
lie imbedded.

After the worms have become hardened in the
formalin, they may be opened, and then it will
be seen that all the organs have become almost
ossified. The ducts will be very brittle, but they
may be put in separate bottles for observation.
Also, the ducts of those dissected before harden-
ing may be kept and shown to better advantage

MOUNTING MILLERS.

In order to have millers perfect when mounted, it is necessary to prepare them as soon as possible after they have accomplished their life's work,— by coupling, and the female depositing her eggs. Have ready a quart fruit-jar, or a perfectly close wooden or tin box. Tie up in a rag a piece of iodide of potassium, and put it in the box or jar. It is well to have the *least* moisture on it, so that it may give off odor. Drop the millers into the box or jar. They will not live an hour. There is another way, which seems more cruel, but does not let them live so long to suffer. Select the millers always in *pairs*, male and female. Have those you want to operate on in a box convenient. Take one at a time. Have the hypodermic syringe ready and filled with the medicated water used for the worms. Place the miller on a piece of pasteboard, and hold it in place by pressing on it very lightly with one finger of the left hand. Take the syringe in the right hand, and inject a few drops of the fluid, inserting the needle in the anus. Lay it aside, and take another and treat it in the same manner, and so on till all are operated on. By that time the first will be dead, if directions have been followed. It is best to handle with the nippers, when it can be done, as the down or feathers of the millers should be preserved whole as much as possible. If you take those from the potassium, take them out with nippers one by one as you operate, and inject a drop or two of the liquid. Have some sterilized cotton convenient, so as to absorb any moisture that may come from the millers.

Have ready as many mounting-cases as you have millers. They are made as described. For ten millers take ten pieces of heavy pasteboard or very light wood, 2 x 2½ inches. Have a piece of very smooth slat 42 inches long and 1 x ½ inch wide. Saw this up into twenty two-inch pieces. Tack two of these pieces on the pasteboards, on either side, so that there will be a groove of one half-inch in the center between the side-pieces. Tack them on the short way of the pieces. Into this groove the body of the miller fits so as to leave the wings horizontal with the body. This is the proper way to mount the silk-miller.

Put a little sterilized cotton in the groove. Have library paste at hand. Take a piece of tarlatan, and cut strips a little more than an inch wide and about three inches long. Fasten one end of the strip to the left side of the case, on the upper end. Then take up the miller and arrange it in the groove, with the wings extending horizontally as far as possible, and in line with the top of the case, and on a level with the body of the miller. Then bring the tarlatan over the left wing tightly. (*Do not drag* it over.) Then hold it down with one finger while you pass it over, and fasten down with paste the other end of the tarlatan. Arrange the right wing in the same way. See that the body is perfectly straight and natural Arrange the head so that the feelers will be in line with the wings and yet in the proper curve. Take fine nippers and draw the feet out so that at least two may be seen more, if possible. If the wings have slipped out of place, take a fine needle, and through the tarlatan put them in place, and then hold them there by sticking a naturalist's pin through the upper part of the wing, fastening it to the case.

All this work requires the greatest exactness and care. When everything has been done as directed, lay away the little cases in a shallow box or on a large pasteboard to dry. This will require a month or six weeks. Put some mothballs in amongst the cases, and beware of ants, mice, or rats, for they will, if possible, get at them and utterly destroy them.

The cocoonery should always be provided with a thermometer and barometer. A dish of salt will in some measure answer the place of a barometer, as if the salt shows much moisture, the air should be dried.

MULBERRY TREES.

The foundation of silk-production is the mulberry tree, as from it is developed the best quality, as well as the greatest quantity, of silk, in proportion to the amount of labor expended.

There are many varieties of the mulberry. Each kind produces a quality of silk corresponding to the quality of leaf-food coming from the tree. Some yield a very coarse silk, and others an exceedingly fine quality. Some yield a larger quantity of silk to the pound of leaves, than others. But all varieties of the mulberry yield more and better silk to the quantity of leaves, than any other plant or tree, so far as yet known to silk-culturists.

Silkworms require food containing four substances; viz , fibrous, resinous, saccharine, and watery. The fibrous holds the leaves intact while the worms are feeding; the saccharine and watery substances nourish the worm; and the resinous substance yields the silk.

In proportion as these substances are contained in the leaf-food, they are valuable.

The white mulberry, in all its varieties, is considered the best silk-producer. Its principal varieties are the *Morus Japonica, Morus alba,*

Morus Moretti, Morus rosa, Morus alba proper, and the *Morus multicaulis.*

The *Morus Japonica* is generally cultivated in silk countries, as it yields more silk to the pound of leaves, than any other, giving one pound of cocoons to every twelve pounds of leaves. It leaves out early in the spring, grows rapidly, and retains its foliage late in the autumn. The leaves are large and heavy. It is easy to propagate it from cuttings. The fruit is of little consequence. But few berries attain perfection, as they fall off before ripening.

The *Morus Moretti* grows tall and straight. It has abundant foliage, but yields only one pound of cocoons to every fourteen pounds of leaves. The leaves are not very large, and are thin and oval in shape. They are smooth on both upper and lower surface. This tree is largely cultivated along the Alps — in the south of France, and in Italy. It makes a beautiful ornamental tree.

The *Morus rosa* has a leaf shaped like the rose leaf, and very shiny. The branches extend more laterally than most varieties. It bears some fruit, of a pinkish tint, not of any commercial value. Some silk-growers prefer this tree, as it does not contain so much of the watery substance as many others. The leaves better sus-

tain the worm. It does not grow so rapidly as
others, and is slow to send out new branches
when pruned. It yields about one pound of
cocoons to fourteen pounds of leaves.

The *Morus alba* proper is the stock from which
the *Japonica, rosa,* and *Moretti* have been produced by cutting and grafting. In all the silk-
growing countries of Europe it is considered a
standard tree. It yields one pound of cocoons
to every fourteen to sixteen pounds of leaves.

The *Morus multicaulis* is a native of the Philip-
pine Islands. The leaves are very large. It
grows very rapidly, and sends out a multitude
of branches, but it requires eighteen pounds of
leaves to make one pound of cocoons. As it
leaves out early in the spring-time, the leaves do
very nicely for the first two ages of the silkworm.

The *Morus nigra,* or Persian mulberry, is a
fine hardy tree, that will thrive even in a cold
climate. It flourishes greatly in southern California. It bears rich, large black fruit, valuable
as a marketable product. The leaves are of
medium size, coarse as the grape leaf, which
they resemble. They are dark green on the
upper side, and covered on the under side with a
kind of white down. In Asiatic countries they
feed this leaf to silkworms as a medicine. In
California it has proved a valuable food all

through the fifth age. Worms develop more rapidly when fed on the leaves of this tree; and the silk made from it seems stronger and coarser than that from any of those mentioned. It is very advisable to have a good proportion of these trees in every mulberry orchard.

Within the past thirty years many varieties of mulberry trees have been imported into California. Some of these varieties, through long neglect and want of cultivation, have sadly degenerated, and now are not good food for the silkworm. Notably of this class is a species of black, which has a smooth, dark green leaf, that seems quite oily as picked from the tree. Worms refuse to eat this when they can get anything else.

The weeping mulberry is of little value as a silk-producer, and Downing's Everbearing is no better. They both bear fruit abundantly, but the leaves are very thin, and have not much of silk-substance in them.

Most of the trees mentioned will grow readily from cuttings. Some will attain a growth of ten feet in a single season. Cuttings may be put in the ground every month in the year in southern California. During the later months of the year they will not grow so rapidly, but they will take root and grow, if properly cared for, and watered so that the ground will always be moist above where the slip ends. If the soil gets dry above that point, the sap, or life, becomes dry, and the cutting will surely die. It is better to propagate mulberry trees by cuttings, than from seed, as ' they come into use much sooner. One pound of seed will give out five thousand trees, but it will be two or three years before the leaves should be picked for feeding.

Last of all trees named for silk-production, and yet best of all, is the "CATTANEO" mulberry, which is a native of Italy. This tree has been acknowledged by scientists interested in silk-culture to be the best, because it contains the most nutriment, and is best adapted to develop the silk-glands of the worm. Also, it is said to grow very much more rapidly; yet it requires no better soil, nor any more care, than other trees. It is largely used in most of the European, as well as in the Asiatic, silk-growing countries. Many thousands of these trees were imported into California when the silk business attracted so much attention in this state. It is said that a Cattaneo mulberry tree eight years old will yield as many leaves as one of the common species at forty years of age. It is also known that this tree does not require to be grafted, and therefore the leaves may be taken from it the first year after planting.

There are three ways of planting the mulberry tree.

1. As a forest tree, when ninety to one hundred and fifty trees may be planted to the acre, and the trees be allowed to grow tall, as well as to branch out laterally. This style of planting involves more labor in gathering the leaves, than any other.

2. Trees may be planted as a mulberry grove, when twelve hundred trees may be put on one acre. In this style the trees are never allowed to grow tall, nor have they room to spread very far, as the branches are constantly clipped off, giving room for others, and still others, to take the places of those cut off. In this case it is much easier to get at the leaves, nor are they so liable to be battered by the wind.

The Chinese never let their trees grow more than three years, as they constantly replace the old with new slips, and dig up the old.

The third style is the mulberry hedge. This is an especially good way for early spring feeding, as the leaves come out earlier, and are better sheltered from the winds by the multitude of branches.

CULTIVATION.

Whatever the order of planting, all mulberries should be well and regularly cultivated, fertilized occasionally, and irrigated when the soil demands it.

A loose, sandy soil is best for the mulberry of

all kinds   But even this is not enough. Attention should be given to the soil, and what the
soil most lacks should be supplied in the kind of
fertilizer used.   All the waste from the cocooneries makes an excellent fertilizer.

Aside from and in addition to the regular
mulberry orchard, many trees can be put in odd
places round the barn-yards, and in the corners
of the fences by the roadside.   Every mulberry
tree planted in southern California should be
made to verify the name given to the tree centuries ago by the Chinese; viz, the "*Golden* tree."
Yes; every tree represents money, as well as
pleasure

PRUNING

The pruning of the mulberry tree is a very
important item in the production of silk.   There
is as great a difference in style and manner of
pruning the several kinds of trees as there is in
their general appearance.   However, all kinds
should be kept at all times in as symmetrical
shape as possible.   The *Japonica*, for instance,
will bear to be pruned from three to six times a
year, while the *rosa*, being more slow of growth,
cannot be made to give out so many crops of
leaves.   Pruning and picking leaves so nearly
represent the same work, that they may be
treated under the same heading

There is nothing more detrimental to the best

results from any mulberry tree, than to pick off the leaves and leave the long branchlets bare of foliage, except the young, tender leaves at the extreme end. When this is done, the strength of the tree goes to wood-fiber, and the limb continues to grow in length, and to send out leaves at the extreme end, while the spaces between the leaf-joints become longer and longer, and the leaves at the end are less and less in size and more inferior in quality. This should be avoided in all orchards; as the closer together the leaves grow, the better. They are less liable to become battered by the wind, and they seem to shield each other from the scorching rays of the noonday sun.

The better way is to cut off the branchlets just two leaves from the branch, and cut off the two leaves a half-inch from the leaf. In due time new buds will shoot out where the leaves were; these in a few weeks will be ready to be treated in the same way, and so on for three or four times during the season, or as often as the trees will bear picking without injury. This mode of treatment will keep the trees in beautiful shape all the time.

It is not advisable to take off more than half or one third of the branchlets at one time. Take off the longest branchlets each time, and keep on, so that there will be a constant supply of leaves for the continuous hatchings of the worms.

If it be found necessary to prune trees to prevent them growing too tall, this should be done in the fall or winter, when the sap is down.

When it is found advisable to have leaves picked in advance for a day or two, it is quite necessary to spray or sprinkle them with pure water. A whisk dipped in water lightly will do very nicely. (But do not do as the Chinese and Japanese; viz., take a mouthful of ¯water and spurt it out on the leaves.) Each time you sprinkle, toss up the leaves from the bottom, so that all may come in contact with the moisture. Then cover them over with old newspapers or clean cloths. When leaves are shipped from a distance, they should be ordered in clean sacks, not in boxes. They should be picked before sunrise, and put up before the coolness of the night passes off from them. When leaves are heated, after picking as high as 80° F., they are very apt to engender disease in the worms. From fourteen hundred to eighteen hundred pounds of leaves will feed forty thousand worms (one ounce of eggs) through all the ages.

LEAVES. — HOW TO CARE FOR THEM.

It is well to have on hand at all times enough leaves to feed four or five times,

It will not do at any time to feed either wet or dusty leaves, and it is much better not to feed them wilted, as the worms crawl over them, but do not like to eat them. If the leaves are dusty, the branches should be plunged in a tank or large tub of clean water, and then shaken so that the water runs off.

Leaves should always be gathered in the morning, before the sun's rays have at all heated them. There is more sap in leaves gathered in the morning, and they are therefore much better for the worms; also, they keep very much better. When gathered, they should be at once taken to the room where they are to be stored, and shaken out of the sacks or baskets in which they were gathered. Then if dry (i. e., not moist with dew), they should be sprinkled lightly with pure water and tossed up with the hand. A clean whisk-broom is good to sprinkle with. If the branches are very long, it is best to cut them about eighteen inches, as they will fit on the trays much more conveniently.

It is never best to pick leaves off trees, and leave long, bare branchlets with a few leaf buds at the extreme end. It is better to cut off the branch two buds from the trunk or large branch; these two or three leaves may be taken off. In a very short time young branchlets will come out, and grow as long as the first, with fresh and tender leaves all along.

The following table will give some idea of the

quantity of leaves required for a given number of worms in their respective ages

One ounce of eggs will hatch out 40,000 worms, and will require —

The first   age, 4 days,   5 pounds daily
The second age, 5 days, 10 pounds daily
The third   age, 5 days, 25 pounds daily
The fourth age, 5 days, 60 pounds daily.
The fifth   age, 8 days, 150 pounds daily.

Average quantity, first age, 16 to 20 daily.
Average quantity, second age,   50 daily
Average quantity, third   age,   125 daily
Average quantity, fourth age,   300 daily
Average quantity, fifth   age, 1,200 daily.

Total   1,695

About two fifths of this is waste.

This amount of leaves will vary according to the kind of leaves supplied and the care taken in feeding them   Old worms, or those in the fourth and fifth age, will not eat the young, tender leaves, that alone are fit to feed worms in the first and second ages. When leaves have become crisp or brittle, through age, they are not good for worms of any age. The *quota* of silk from such leaves is very small

The motto of every silk-grower should be, "*The best of everything*" Best trees, best leaves, best worms, best cocoons, best silk, — best *pay*.

MISCELLANEOUS NOTES ON SILK.

Note 1

The first silk-mill on this continent was erected in 1810, in Mansfield, Connecticut. Now there are over nine hundred silk-mills or factories in the United States, and some in Canada.

The world's silk-production is more than 11,706 tons per annum

Note 2.

The gold and silver spider are both found in Rhodesia, South Africa.

The gold spider spins its web (not in cocoon) of golden thread, and lets it float from the trees. Sometimes these webs are twenty feet long; they float loosely, glistening in the sunshine, till they strike other branches. Then they stretch from branch to branch, or from tree to tree, making a gorgeous appearance in the tropical sun The fiber of this web is of great fineness.

The silver spider spins a less beautiful web It is spun from bush to bush, or from one tree to another, but is not left to float loosely It is not so strong as the golden spider's thread, though very beautiful.

These spiders live on flies, which are very abundant in that country.

Note 3.

A farmer of Mitcham, Australia, has discovered that the mulching of fruit trees with eucalyptus leaves is a sure preventive of blight, fungi, and insect pests. He says he has trees so treated, which are entirely free from pests, while others close-by, not so treated, are almost worthless. It might be well to use some around mulberry trees to prevent any insects.

Hundreds of years ago, and ever since, the mulberry tree is spoken of as being always free from indigenous pests of all kinds. But experience has shown that if they are in close proximity to trees covered with scale, the scale will be carried either by the wind or by insects, and will rest on the mulberry.

It is best, therefore, not to have scale-breeding trees near the mulberry grove. It is well to have a eucalyptus hedge round each grove. The leaves can then be used for mulching and for fumigating the cocooneries.

Note 4

WEIGHTED SILKS.

Sometimes ninety per cent of the material (i. e., silk goods) is of foreign substance. At the present day the practice of "weighting" silks by means of astringent extracts, salts of tin, silicate, and phosphate of soda, and a variety of other substances, all more or less injurious to the wear of the fabric, has reached such a height, that it is seriously affecting the trade. This is especially the case as regards black silks, but fabrics of other colors suffer in the same manner.

It used to be said that a silk dress or a silk handkerchief would last a lifetime, and this is almost true where one can obtain the pure silk. But in much of the fabric sold as silk at the present day there is not more than ten to twelve per cent of real pure silk, all the rest being extraneous matter applied to the fiber in the deceptive process of "weighting."

Pure silk, when burned, leaves a quantity of ash, which is always considered less than one per cent, but the ash left by some weighted silks has been found to amount to as much as forty-eight per cent of the weight of the fabric.

The extraneous substances to which we have alluded are caused to adhere to the fiber by passing the skeins of silk through hot baths of tannin, extracts of tin, salts, salts of iron, antimony, potash, etc., and it has been found that when a silk heavily charged with such substances is heated, it will not burn with flame, but will only smolder away, leaving a very large amount of ash behind.

But these weighted silks are, however, of so
combustible a nature, that some have been
known to take fire spontaneously, — a result due
to the gradual decomposition of the substances
used for weighting, — and disastrous fires have
been traced to this cause Spontaneous combus-
tion is liable to break out, — more especially in
black silks, that are stored in warm, dry places.

Note 5.

A very curious silk industry is carried on in
Spain since the people became too indolent and
careless to manufacture silk into fabrics. The
process is called gut-making, and is described as
follows. When silkworms are all ready to spin,
they take them, and with a sharp instrument cut
off both ends Then they deftly take out both
silk-tubes, — described fully under another heading in this book, — and stretch them to the
fullest extent, — or at least several feet in length,
according as the worm is fine and vigorous, or
puny from being ill fed. They are handled very
carefully as they are unfolded from the convolu-
tions in which they were by nature arranged in
the body of the worm. They are then passed
through several chemical processes or prepara-
tions, that serve to cleanse and strengthen them.
They are then dried and tied together in bundles.

This treatment of the silk gland or tube of the silkworm leaves a strong, fine, elastic filament, which is almost invisible in water. This is why it is so desirable as a fishing-line attachment. This little ending of the fishing-line is what is called the gut-leader. A short piece of this is fastened on the extreme end of the line. Sometimes it is so fastened as to leave both ends free, on which to fasten two hooks. When the line is thrown out into the water, the gut is almost invisible, and the fishes see only the bait on the hook. This they bite, and are at once taken. The strength of the gut is quite sufficient to hold even two fish such as are caught with hook and line. Most of the silkworms now raised in Spain are treated in this way. The gut when prepared in this manner is peddled through the streets of the cities.

The silk-gut is also used in another way. When it has been sterilized, it is used in surgery, as a suture to unite either bones or muscles. It may be left in the wound till the absorbents of the system carry it off, as there is not the slightest danger of blood-poison.

Note 6.

The most advanced nations in silk-culture do most to foster the silk industry among their people a knowledge of the insect to which they owe so much of their national wealth In both France and Italy, it is a part of the education of young ladies. They are taught all the details of the production of silk, from the egg to the reeled silk. There it is considered a most healthful and refreshing change, to pass from the study of books to behold living nature in her strange and wonderful changes,— from apparently repeated deaths to larger and still larger spheres of life and activity

It is a constantly demonstrated fact that nothing is more important as the basis of a solid education, than strict attention to little things For this reason, if nothing else, is the education in the silk industry of great use to the young. The United States is almost the only nation where large manufactures are carried on, where there is not one or more schools of instruction in this special branch of industry, supported by the government. The art of silkworm-rearing is wholly neglected in the system of education in our beloved land, while we have the most superior advantages for the production of silk. This is the groundwork of the lack of interest in the entire business.

France leads the world in the superior style of her textile manufactures. This fact is said to be largely owing to the education of the children in practical schools of learning. Lessons in the every-day life of nature are demonstrated to them, as well as in all the arts and sciences that are brought into use in working one's way through the busy marts of life.

Our manual-training schools are a step in advance, which gives room to hope that these schools will be still further enlarged in all that may better qualify the young to arm themselves to go through life well fitted for all that may come to them on its changeful battle-fields.

Note 7.

"In 1899, the earliest spinning of silk-cocoons was taken to the Chamber of Commerce, March 28, by Mrs. Carrie Williams, who there exhibited as fine large and firm cocoons as can be found at any season of the year. These cocoons were spun by worms hatched in February and matured in March, in a temperature varying from 44° to 75° F. The worms were from $3\frac{1}{2}$ to 4 inches long, and in the most perfect health. The only difference low and uneven temperature seems to make is, that it prolongs the life to about forty days, instead of thirty. Hundreds of other worms, just as fine, will be spinning in a few days, and may be seen by those interested. Also, worms of all ages." — *San Diego Union.*

ₜNote 8.

Many unreliable statements are made by a great variety of writers in regard to the profits to be derived from the silk industry; also, concerning the nature, care, feeding, size, length of life, etc. I give below an example of this exaggerated style of writing, from the Student's Cyclopedia, page 1203 —

" . . Silkworms are one quarter of an inch at first, and three inches when ready to spin, which is about eight weeks. One ounce of eggs will produce one hundred pounds of cocoons, which will yield one pound of silk. About twenty-two million pounds of silk is produced in the world annually."

Actual experience shows that, as a rule, silkworms are not more than one eighth to three eighths of an inch when first hatched from the shells. Some especially fine worms may be three eighths of an inch. When ready to spin, unless they have been very sadly neglected as to food, they are $3\frac{3}{4}$ to 4 inches long, and the lifetime is from 25 to 32 days.

Statistics on textile production show that more than thirty-five million pounds of raw silk are produced in the world annually.

One ounce of eggs will yield from 35,000 to

40,000 silkworms, and these will spin 175 to 200 pounds of dry cocoons. Ten to twelve pounds of these cocoons will, when fresh, give off one pound of silk. When dry, it will require 2 to $3\frac{1}{2}$ pounds. So we see from an absolute knowledge of facts, that instead of one ounce of silk-eggs yielding but one pound of silk, they will give sixteen to twenty-two pounds.

It seems a pity that such erroneous statements should find place in books that are read by the young, as they give false ideas of the great possibilities of our great and growing industries.

Note 9.

On the authority of Mr. Frank Cheney, president of the Silk Manufacturers' Association of the United States, I give the following statement: "One pound of reeled silk will make from five to fifty yards of silk goods." (See Revision of the Tariff, for A D 1890, page 606.)

The fifty yards would, of course, be very light gauzes; the five yards would be the heaviest drapery. Ten to twelve yards of gros-grain can be made from one pound, so that it is safe to state that a very good silk dress can be made from one pound of reeled silk.

Note 10.

History of Product of One Miller in 1895 (*June*). — One miller laid more than four hundred eggs, and these hatched out more than four hundred perfect worms, that spun over four hundred perfect cocoons. From these cocoons I selected 150, — 75 males and 75 females. They (the millers) were duly coupled after emerging from their cocoons. The females laid, as nearly as I could estimate, twenty thousand eggs, which I sold for two dollars.

If the whole brood had been left for breeding, the cash returns would have been nearly six dollars from one pair.

Note 10.

Some cocoons raised at Point Loma, San Diego County, in A. D. 1901, reeled off 1,176 yards of silk fiber to the cocoon.

Note 11.

Two and a half pounds of raw silk will make 480 spools of No. A silk, at 5 cents each, that would be $24. At 10 cents each, of course, double that, or $48.

One acre of good mulberry grove will produce about 70 to 110 pounds of reeled silk. Made into spools at the above price, it would bring $2,640.

Note 12.

Our United States cocoons measure more than any foreign cocoons yet recorded.

DISEASES OF SILKWORMS.

Much might be said of the diseases of silk-worms, — the cause and cure. But as the United States have never yet been afflicted in this particular way, it is deemed best to pass the subject lightly over, merely noting a few facts.

Within the last half-century, almost every country where silkworms are reared has been afflicted with a most terrible disease, so that it was feared, at one time, that the silk industry would be entirely swept from the face of the earth. The French government took great interest in this subject, and appointed Pasteur, one of the ablest scientists of his day, to investigate the cause, and, if possible, recommend a cure. He was allowed by the government every possible facility to prosecute his work, and he was also ably assisted by other scientists, who might be named, — Professor Lebert, De Osinio of Italy, Frederick Haberlandt, Emilio Cama, and others; while, later on, Colonel Charles Brady, of Sydney, New South Wales, by patient, persistent study and labor, through many years of experiment, at last overcame the diseases and developed some of the finest breeds of silkworms that have ever been known to the civilized world.

It was all very well, and we would not detract one iota from the honor justly due to these noble scientists, but we deem it most advisable to ward off disease of all kinds, which can assuredly be done by proper care and judicious management. Again I would reiterate what so often has been said : To avoid all manner of disease. Provide suitable quarters and ample room. Feed *abundantly* and *regularly*, with wholesome food Never give either wet or dusty leaves. Keep the temperature even, — 75° to 80° F., night and day. *Then* there will be no need of expending large sums for the services of scientists to explain the cause and recommend the cure of any fatal disease.

The most malignant disease referred to above is pebrin. This first appeared in 1840, at Provinza. It continued to spread throughout Europe and Asia for more than twenty years. Upon scientific investigation this disease proved to be a parasite, that lodged in all parts of the worm, even in the blood and alimentary canal It was also found in the miller, in the wings, the feet, and even in the eyes, and also in the substance of the egg, and attached to the shell. It was also in the chrysalis. These parasites preyed on all parts of the living silkworm, in all ages and stages, and wasted their lives so as to render them absolutely worthless as to the purpose of their creation. The worst feature of this malady was the difficulty in destroying the pests. Neither alcohol nor acids would affect them in the least, and it was proved that they would live for years in water, and become active as soon as removed from the water. If they were thrown out to decay and waste, the germs would so contaminate leaves, if at all near them, that at once the dread disease would be transmitted to new fields to prey upon new subjects. So that it was clearly proved that the only mode of ending this dreadful disease was by *fire;* to burn up *everything* that might in any way have been tainted or contaminated by it.

Worms affected by this disease were observed to grow unequally, to become languid and lose appetite, and often spots would appear on the skin. This disease, like all others, was more manifest in the fourth and fifth ages, than the earlier ages.

Another silkworm disease is "grasserie," or jaundice. In this the worms become very yellow, get soft and limp, and then finally die.

Another disease is called "muscardine." This sometimes proves very destructive. The worms become languid, and suddenly die, and in a short time become stiff and discolored. If they

SILK IN CHINA.

In looking back over the world's history, we find that so little is known by the general public regarding this the third great textile industry of the world, that it is deemed best here to give a very brief outline of its rise, growth, and present *status*.

The silk industry originated in China. Old traditions mention it as far back as 2700 B C. In those early days the royal household cared for the silkworms and made silk into fabrics Reference is made by Chinese poets to the silkworm and the mulberry tree as early as 1000 years B C. For centuries it was deemed a capital offense to export eggs, or even let it be known how these gorgeous robes were obtained.

From China, sericulture gradually spread to Persia, and finally to Europe About A. D. 530, two monks went over from Turkey to China, as missionaries; and during their labors carefully noted how the Chinese cared for the silkworm, as well as how they handled the frail threads of silk composing the cocoons. They managed to secure a quantity of silk-eggs, put them into hollow canes, and using these as walking-canes, they walked out of China, carrying with them the great national secret. They went direct to Constantinople, and presented their canes with their valuable contents to the Emperor Constantine.

As early as the twelfth century, silk-weaving was a recognized industry in England. The silk then used was obtained from Syria, in cloth. These fabrics were unraveled, and the silk shreds rewoven with other materials. It is said they were more beautiful than at the first. This practice is mentioned by Aristotle.

When cotton was introduced from India, about A. D 1260, owing to its cheapness, it in a great measure superseded silk, which had been a flourishing industry for four thousand years. In 1644, the silk industry had retained only enough activity to supply local demands and the government requirements. However, intercourse with other nations has revived the silk industry in China, so that at the present time silk is produced in every province. The best silk comes from Che Kiang, especially from its northwest corner But even this does not equal Italian or French silk. Some full-grown trees will yield seventy to one hundred pounds of leaves But, as a rule, the Chinese do not allow the mulberry tree to grow more than five or six feet high. They live for fifty years in China. In some

European countries there are many mulberry trees three hundred years old.

The Chinese are very systematic about the pruning of their trees. When the young trees are planted, they are set five or six feet apart, and cut down to eighteen inches above-ground. When the new shoots appear, they are all cut off, except two. Each year, the wood of the previous year is cut off in feeding the worms. Only two buds are left on each stem from year to year. This style of cutting and pruning gradually gives the tree the shape of an umbrella.

The Chinese continue to reel and weave as they did thousands of years ago.

There are about two hundred looms employed in weaving silk and velvet for the imperial household. In A. D. 1889, on account of the Emperor's marriage, there were three million dollars' worth of silk goods manufactured. The kind of silk made for royalty is forbidden to all other classes of citizens. Those who weave for the royalty of China get higher wages than other weavers. Women and girls who weave ribbons get eight to ten cents a day, with board (boiled rice). Men get fifteen to twenty cents a day, and the same board.

There are two principal kinds of silk manufactured in China. The "ling," which has a thin glossy surface; and the "hung," which means an imperial fabric In making these silks, there are three or four men employed on each loom, and their united labor only turns out twelve to sixteen feet of silk a day. The best silk sells for sixty to ninety cents a yard

Raw silk is made from worms fed on a mixture of wild and tame mulberry leaves, —.eight parts of wild and two of tame. This kind of silk is also used for the woof of pongee silk and satin.

At Nankin there are seven or eight thousand looms employed in making satin. These are the richest satins woven in China It is a kind of damask interwoven with a thread of gold.

Like all other works of art in China, the weaving of silk is an individual matter, as a rule. Each one spins and weaves and dyes his own silks. Hence there is little division of labor, and little opportunity to invest capital in manufactories. However, there are several filatures in China, where foreign machinery is employed in reeling and weaving silks.

In China, silk is a common article of attire, and both sexes take pride in arraying themselves in gorgeous robes of gay colors. The actual amount of silk used in China seems to be beyond computation It is safely estimated that more than double the quantity of silk is used at home that there is exported.

In A. D. 1890 there was exported from China alone about 21,123,600 pounds of silk. Double this amount would be 42,247,200 pounds. This would allow a fraction more than two ounces of silk to each of the 300,000,000 inhabitants of the Celestial Empire.

REARING SILKWORMS IN CHINA.

The Chinese have ten general rules for the rearing of silkworms.

1. The eggs while on paper must be kept cool

2. When the worms hatch out, they must be kept warm.

3. When molting, they must be left without food.

4. During the intervals between the molts, they must be well supplied with food

5. They must not be placed too close together, nor too far apart.

6. During their sleeps they should be kept dark and warm; after they have cast their skins, cool, with plenty of light.

8. For a little time after molting they should be sparsely fed. When they are full grown, they should never be without fresh food

9. Their eggs should be laid close together, but not heaped upon one another.

10. Wet, withered, or dusty leaves should never be given to silkworms in any age.

In the province of Canton there are two special kinds of worms. One kind hatches once a year; the other kind, seven times a year.

The Chinese have many foolish superstitions about silkworms, which are not worth mentioning. They weigh the worms in their last sleep, and estimate that 1 pound of worms will eat about 15 pounds of leaves, and spin 1½ pounds of silk.

The health of the worms is indicated by their manner of eating and general appearance. If they eat ravenously, they are well, also if the skin be full and shiny. When the joints look bluish or greenish, or the worms look a dead white, they should be destroyed.

Leaves must never be over-heated after picking.

The best and most healthy worms are hatched about the middle of April, and mature in twenty-seven days. The worms are put to spin in bundles of straw, on mats, about one hundred in each bundle. When taken out, the best and cleanest are reserved for the finest silk.

A skillful Chinese can reel by hand from one pound ten ounces to one pound fourteen ounces a day.

SILK IN JAPAN.

It is not generally known when silk was first introduced into Japan. But since early in the fifth century of the Christian era the people of Japan have been enthusiastic workers in the production and manufacture of silk. It is recorded of them, that the government at one time had to enact restraining laws, lest other branches of industry be wholly neglected. The further planting of the mulberry was forbidden, and the use of silk goods was confined to certain classes of society.

A kindly, patient, intelligent people, the Japanese seem especially adapted to manage the silkworm. And no people ever reaped more substantial reward for their manipulation of this business than they did, when the terrible silk-worm disease almost wiped out the entire silk industry in Europe and Asia, some years ago. At that time one of the largest ocean steamers, the Delhi, was chartered to convey from Japan, to Europe, a full cargo of silk-eggs, the insured value of which was over half a million pounds sterling ($2,500,000).

For some years Japan exported annually $4,701,400 worth of eggs alone, besides large quantities of reeled and raw silk. These large profits were the result of the annual silkworm, as Japan does not raise more than one or two crops of silk a year. The Japanese white silk is the finest silk in the world As a people, they have vastly improved their machinery within the past forty years. Their treatment of the silkworm is more scientific than that of the Chinese, as they are more advanced in all the arts and sciences of the age

They have to be very careful of the silkworms, and protect them from currents of the outside atmosphere, as the climate is very changeful, and at times severely cold

The Japanese prune their trees very closely every year. They propagate largely by layering,—i e, they lay down branches, or long shoots from the main body of the tree, then cover them with the soil. They soon take root, and shoot up sprouts, which are in due time transplanted and given more room.

Besides silk in all conditions,—from the waste silk to the finished fabric,—the Japanese export mulberry trees of the best kind.

When the winter weather has really set in, those who are engaged in the propagation of eggs take them and immerse them in water just down to the freezing-point, where they let them remain a short time, then let them drain off, and finally dry them thoroughly before packing them away for the coming season. This may be their method of weeding out all the delicate seed.

SILK IN HUNGARY.

In Hungary, the government provides for the reeling of cocoons. They buy the cocoons from the producers, for two thirds of the market value, because they furnish them with the eggs and the leaves. The government owns large plantations of mulberry trees, and forbids the sale of eggs.

Other European countries raise more or less silk, both for home use and exportation, but we have not space here to enter into detail of any but the most important:

SILK IN FRANCE.

During the thirteenth century an attempt was made to introduce the silk industry into France. But little progress was made until about 1521, when King Henry IV encouraged the industry, and the people engaged in the planting and care of the white mulberry tree. It is recorded that the first mulberry tree planted at that time is still growing.

The industry was still further encouraged by Louis XIV.; and both the production and manufacture of the new fabric increased in value till the Revolution, during the eighteenth century. This upturning of the nation's industrial, social, and religious life nearly obliterated the silk industry.

Napoleon Bonaparte proved a benefactor to the French people, in that he greatly encouraged the silk business, and again it was on the road to prosperity, when, in A. D. 1850, the dreadful disease so contagious swept over Europe as does a plague, and almost wiped out the silk business of the world   Again the government of France rose to the aid of her people, and appointed the noted scientist Pasteur to search out and apply remedies for the stay of the fearful disease.   His system was based on very exact microscopical examination of the eggs and the millers. This system proved to be a very expensive addition to the silk business.

Signore Surani, of Milan, Italy, was the first to put this system on a commercial basis. He had the largest establishment in the world. He employed 3,000 hands during the coupling season, and 750 scientists for the critical examination of the eggs and millers with the most perfect instruments.

None of these expenses need ever be incurred in the United States, because with our salubrious climate, and our continuous supplies of the best of foods, it is quite needless that disease should ever be allowed to even appear in our beloved land.

Silk-manufacture is carried on to a very high degree of perfection in Lyons and other large cities of France; but the United States are fast overtaking them, both in style and quality of silk weaves.

The production of silk has been on the decrease in France for a number of years. Disease still lingers in the agricultural districts, and proves very discouraging to the peasantry.

SILK IN GREAT BRITAIN.

From the time of Edward III. until the year
1824, the English government sought from time
to time to promote the silk-weaving industry by
acts of Parliament, and the imposition of duties
upon manufactured silks. However, these acts
did not tend to promote the silk business in
England. They have also made many attempts
to produce silkworms in England, but the coolness and almost constant humidity of the climate
forbid its success from time to time. King
James II., in A. D. 1605, spent $4,675 in planting
mulberry trees round his palace. He offered
packets of mulberry seed to any who would sow
them, for the purpose of raising silkworms. This
royal patronage rendered the tree so popular,
that to-day in many private gardens in England
may be seen mulberry trees planted in the seven-
teenth century About this time, one hundred
thousand of the black mulberry species were
brought over from France, and planted in England and Wales

In 1669, King James strongly advocated silk-
production in his kingdom, but with little
success This same monarch ordered the planting of the mulberry in the American colonies,

and sought to enforce the silk industry by fines and premiums. The Huguenots brought the culture to South Carolina, and at that time some silk was manufactured. Some of these old trees are said to be still living in South Carolina, where much interest is now being manifested in the silk industry.

When, in 1734, the South Sea Bubble enlisted so much English capital, Oglethorpe planted the mulberry in Georgia, and in due time he produced raw silk, and sent as a present to Queen Caroline of England eight pounds of his silk. From this silk Charles II. wore a robe and hose at his coronation.

While the colonies were yet under British rule, premiums were bestowed and penalties inflicted, hoping thereby to fix the silk industry in the new possessions, for the treasury of England complained of the enormous drain on her exchequer by the importation of raw silk to supply her numerous silk manufactories About this time, a charter was granted to a London company to take African negroes to the colonies to engage in the cultivation of tobacco. This act of the government killed out all the interest in silk that had been awakened, notwithstanding the fact that the silk produced in the colonies was quoted at "two shillings" a pound more

than any that had been imported. A large
filature was established in Savannah This fact
encouraged many women to continue the production of silk; but, very unfortunately, this was
burned, and with it large quantities of raw and
reeled silk. Soon followed the Revolution. The
fearful struggle of the century, when the colonies
threw off the yoke of the "mother country," and
being but young and poor, their first inhabitants
had no time to look for the luxuries of life.
Daily bread called for their utmost ambition,
and in supplying this all their energies were
engrossed, and the silkworm and its work were
lost sight of, and almost forgotten. With the
peace that followed the Revolution, came the
cotton-gin. Cotton and slave-labor combined to
keep back for a time all efforts in silk-production

In 1825, "The British, Irish, and Colonial Silk
Company" was organized, with a capital stock of
five million dollars, to introduce silk-culture into
Ireland. To promote the interests of this company, the celebrated work on silk and silkworms,
by Dandola, the Italian savant, was translated
into English. This company failed for want of
practical knowledge of the necessary requirements of the silkworm They understood neither
the tree nor the worms. Notwithstanding the
failure of this large company, fine silk has been

produced in Britain, and the loss of silkworms from deaths is recorded at only three per cent. Want of proper management has been, and still is, the *greatest* barrier against silk-culture. It is not enough to know simply that silkworms eat mulberry leaves, and in due time convert a portion of them into silk fiber. *No.* The leaves must be maintained in a perfectly healthy condition, and administered in proper way, at proper times.

The work is so fascinating, and the demand for silk so fully assured in all civilized countries, that people without means are often tempted to begin the work, when they have not sufficient capital to make the provision that is necessary in the first stages of this, as it is in any, business.

SILK-CULTURE IN ITALY.

Silk was introduced into Italy early in this century, when Florence was the center of the manufacturing interests.

For a long time the production, as well as the manufacture, of silk has been the chief wealth of Italy, not only of the people, but also of the government.. Realizing the importance of instructing the people in the management of the silkworm, that they might by intelligent care ward off disease, in 1871 there was a royal decree issued to establish an experimental station at Padua. The Italian government, and the city and Chamber of Commerce of Padua, bore the expense of the institution. The objects of the station are,—

1. To study the raising of silkworms under the best conditions, and experiment with the products thereof.

2. To study the feeding of silkworms, by means of physiological and chemical experiments.

3. To study the diseases of the silkworms, and the mulberry tree.

4. To produce and distribute healthy silkworm eggs for silk-growers.

5. To experiment with new varieties of eggs, as well as with other articles that concern the menagerie.

6. To undertake all such studies and experiments as might be useful to sericulture.

7. To give the greatest possible publicity to all matters connected with the sericultural industry in the kingdom of Italy.

This station has done inestimable service for sericulture, it having granted (within a few years) 250 diplomas to pupils, who at once were given places in sericultural observatories, where their knowledge was freely spread among silk-growers.

In all countries where the silk business has succeeded, the government has lent its aid, as well as its encouragement in various ways.

Florence, Italy, early became interested in the silk business. The government, seeing this, in order to insure its continued success, made a law, that every peasant in the province of Tuscany should plant at least five mulberry trees on the land he cultivated

While Italy very largely produces cocoons and reeled silk, her manufactured silks are not up to the standard of other silk-producing countries of Europe; yet she annually exports about fifty million dollars' worth of silk goods of various grades.

Of the silk-eggs used in Italy, about ninety-six per cent are brought from Japan These eggs cost sixty thousand dollars per ton, and the average import is seventy to eighty tons per annum.

Silk is the most valuable product of Italy, the annual average being fifty million dollars' worth Lombardy is the richest province of Italy in silk-production. Eleven thousand tons of cocoons are produced there, valued at one thousand dollars a ton. Italy produces about one third of the silk of the world.

In A. D. 1892, Italy produced $34,492,500 worth of cocoons. In A D. 1878, Italy had 230 silk factories, with 2,100,000 spindles, giving employment to 16,000 men. There were also 120,-000 women and 76,000 children employed, attending to silkworms.

A Glimpse at Italian Silk-culture as it is Carried on To-day, in Contrast with What It Might be in This Climate and Country, as Represented in This Book.

The gentleman who gave this information is a native of the city of Verona, Italy, and his brother and brother's son carry on the silk industry as herein described. They own two farms of about 350 acres, near the city of Verona, in the province of Lombardy, in the northern part of Italy. It is sheltered on the north and east, and partly on the west, by the Alps, and branches of this range of mountains. The total area of the valley is about 125 by 175 miles. So

it will be readily seen how great and sudden
changes of temperature are liable to occur at any
time during the silk season. Those chilling
winds swooping down from the snow-capped
mountains sometimes destroy the whole crop of
silkworms in the valleys. When these mis-
fortunes occur, the entire crop of silk is lost for
the year, as (there the season is but seven weeks)
they have no eggs in storage, and there are none
in market

Should such a thing occur in our glorious
land, if the people were engaged in silk-culture,
there would be only a loss of the one crop of
worms and the leaves injured by the storm.   In
two or three weeks the leaves would be replaced
by another crop, as tender, fresh, and abundant
as the first, and another brood of worms taken
from cold-storage would grow and thrive, and in
an incredibly short time would fill the place of
those that perished. But such storms have
never yet occurred here.

On these farms are a number of tenant-houses,
of stone, grouped together as a village, with a
church in the center, as is always the case in
Italy. The church is the best building. Most
of the houses are two stories high, built without
any attempt at architectural beauty of design or
finish; hence they have a dreary, uninviting

appearance. These houses are the homes of the laboring classes.

Wages are very low. The wants of the peasantry are few, and not very well supplied. They have no home luxuries, and few indeed of what we call the comforts of life. Their food consists largely of some kind of coarse meal, which they cook in some way two or three times a week, and then they eat it with sour wine. They have no means of heating their houses, save one large fireplace, and even this they are unable to supply with fuel, as wood is very dear. It is quite customary when mothers see their infants shivering with cold, to take them out to the stables where the stock is kept, that they may there feel the warmth generated by living bodies.

The landlords supply everything for their tenants, and they work partly on shares, always seeking to retain the lion's share for themselves.

As well as supplying all material to work with, the land-owners have to keep everything in repair. They also irrigate, and this is an absolute necessity to success in any line of agriculture. Their entire water system is in the hands of an English syndicate, and they charge enormously for irrigation.

When the tenants are not busy with silk, they are engaged in other lines of work. They cultivate some fruit and raise stock for market. To accomplish this (i. e , to fatten stock), every particle of waste from the cocooneries is saved, the parts of dry leaves and tender twigs of the mulberry trees, and even the excrement of the worms, is saved and dried, and stored away in sacks, as grain. It is fed dry, like grain, and proves a wonderful flesh-producer.

The young girls are employed in picking stones off the ground and piling them in heaps. This is their work when not at something else.

When the silk season begins, which is about the 10th of April, everything is life and motion. The landlords buy the silk-seed or eggs (usually from Japan), and deal them out to the household tenants, according to the members of the family who are able to care for the silkworms They hatch them out in small boxes covered with glass, which they put in the sunshine, with paper or cloth over them to keep off the direct sunshine.

When the silk season is fairly inaugurated, these tenants give up their best rooms to the silkworms, while they themselves live in closer quarters At this season, old and young, male and female, are all busy, night and day. They relieve one another during the night. In seven weeks from beginning, the season is all over.

For the worms of the first age they cut the leaves very fine, and for the next two ages, not so small For the two last ages, they do not cut, but feed the branches of the mulberry. They make trays of straw woven into strong wooden frames, nine feet long and three feet wide. These are fastened to two upright posts or stands, and are placed, four or five, one over the other, at equal distance apart. On these trays they place the large worms and feed them with branches, changing them when the *débris* accumulates too much.

It is not at all surprising, that with this mode of raising silkworms, that they have to buy seed every year, for such a style of operating would assuredly tend to develop disease of the worst form.

For the worms to spin, they tie little bundles of twigs or coarse straw together, and lay them on those trays till the worms crawl in and then begin to spin. When the worms have formed the outline of the cocoons, and the branches are as full of the forming cocoons as they think best, they take these branches and stand them up in some quiet place to finish their work

Thus the whole business is carried on in the crudest fashion, and calculated to bring in the most meager results. Nevertheless the landlords find that their profits are much larger from the silk business than from *all other* productions of their landed estates, though the time occupied is only about seven weeks.

The silk season is the busiest, happiest time of

year for all classes. All are anxious to see the outcome. The wealthy ladies are not afraid to use their hoarded pin-money, gambling in stocks of both cocoons and reeled silk

The reels on which these poor peasants reel silk are crude as crude can be, nor can their silk be either as good or as fine in appearance as it might be made with proper care and scientific manipulation. Yet this one small county (Verona) of the province of Lombardy sends out annually five million dollars' worth of silk.

The mulberry trees in this part of Italy are said to be a hundred years old. They are not allowed to grow more than six to ten feet high, and are about twelve feet in circumference They are pruned laterally every year, in the autumn. They have a very gnarly appearance, from having been pruned so many many times.

This gentleman suggested that they try working on a different plan and with better machinery, as also better accommodations for the worms. He was told that it had been tried, but failed; that the tenants were so dishonest, they had to be watched all the time, and this could be done better when they were kept in separate households But even under this management the owners lose many a skein of silk and many a basket of cocoons, for the peasantry well know that silk, to them, is as good as *gold*.

SILK-CULTURE IN AUSTRALIA.

In the year 1825 the Australian Agricultural
Company was organized It⁻was designed to
give encouragement to the production of silk, as
well as other products of the soil. Mulberry
trees were planted, and various attempts made
to establish the silk industry. Through a succes-
sion of years, and in different parts of the island,
different persons attempted to raise silkworms.
Trials and failures followed each other. The
causes of failure were a want of knowledge of the
best locations, as well as not knowing how to
care for the worms. The people were not educated on these special lines of agriculture.

In or about the year 1862, Colonel Charles
Brady took up the matter of silk-culture in Australia and spent many years and much capital
in experimenting on both the silkworms and the
mulberry tree. His continued intelligent labors
were, in one sense at least, fully rewarded. He
succeeded in producing the best races of worms
known to exist in any country, some of which
spun cocoons from which were reeled *eighteen·
hundred* yards of silk fiber..

At the time when the silk disease ravaged
Europe, he obtained some of the best breeds from

all countries, and sought to eliminate disease
from them, and sometimes found it necessary to
destroy the product of an ounce of eggs (40,000),
all except one couple, from which he would
propagate from that respective race. England,
having a faithful, watch care over her colonies,
as well in their industrial development as otherwise, was greatly exercised about the spread of
the silk disease, as its widespread effects seemed
very likely to put a stop to the many silk-looms
that gave employment to so many of her subjects. While there was scarce an ounce of
healthy silk grain to be found in any country
(except Japan), Colonel Brady was faithfully
toiling — battling against the fatal enemy. One
special race that he succeeded in establishing in
perfect health was the *Milanaise,* which race is
now held in very high esteem.

All writers on this subject about that time
gave it as their judgment, that the general cause
of failure was the want of proper calculation in
attempting to rear worms when suitable provision had not been made for their maintenance,
and a knowledge of their requirements had not
been attained This seems to be the reason why
such poor quality of silk comes from India. In
some of the experiments in Australia, the mulberry
trees used were the *Morus multicaulis,* which is

not by any means the best tree for all ages In other cases the groves were set out in localities where the dust from the road in the dry season rested on the leaves, and they failed to wash off the dust. This proved disastrous to silkworms, and very many died from the effects of dust taken into the system. It also is injurious to the worm to come in contact with dust externally, as, their breathing apertures being numerous, they imbibe freely from their surroundings.

Both men and women of note entered into the business of rearing silkworms in the British colony, and with some degree of success,— not, however, as great as would have marked their endeavors, had they gone at the business in a more practical way, and, first of all, counted the cost, and employed only those who understood thoroughly the care of the worms and the cultivation of the mulberry. Colonel Brady made one discovery which had never before been thought of, and which is of incalculable worth to all countries where it is possible to carry out his system. I refer to the continuous hatching out of the silkworm. After long and faithful study with different races and different foods, he discovered that it was possible to have silk-eggs hatch out at all seasons of the year. Next he discovered that it was possible to control these eggs by the use of cold-storage, so that they would not hatch at all times, but only when they were taken from the storage and placed in certain conditions. Whenever leaf-food was ready, then the eggs could be brought by slow degrees to a warm and still warmer temperature, till 70° F. was reached, at which temperature they would hatch in three or four days.

The particulars of this wonderful secret is not given in any of Colonel Brady's writings, that I have yet seen. Neither is it generally known that such a secret has been discovered; as the books—what few there are written on this subject—speak of the silkworm season as only one small portion of the year.

In another chapter in this book I will give a slight account of my experiments, and the results that followed.

The adaptation of Australia to silk-culture was fully demonstrated by the quality of cocoons and the silks that were there produced.

After more than twenty years' faithful work and of scientific experiments, Colonel Charles Brady induced the government of the colony to take hold of the silk business. They seemed more inclined to benefit their own country by the development of silk, than to spread abroad the knowledge acquired at such cost of time and patient experiments.

In 1894, Colonel Brady took thirty trays of living silkworms, also a quantity of live cocoons, to an agricultural exhibition, 280 miles by railroad. They all arrived in perfect condition, and attracted more attention at the exhibit than any one feature represented by those who took part in it. The people were all amazed to see the complete exhibition of the industry from the eggs to the eggs again, as the millers were there laying eggs, and the little worms were hatching out of the previously laid eggs.

Colonel Brady's estimate of the profit of the silk business is that an acre of mulberries properly cared for will yield $75 to $125. This signifies one crop. If, therefore, our California trees will bear three or four crops of leaves, the profits will, of course, be correspondingly greater. The climate of San Diego is very much better than most parts of Australia.

SILK IN THE UNITED STATES.

Ere yet the Stars and Stripes were thought of as a national emblem, or known, save in the mind of the great Jehovah, who has marked us as a people for whom he has reserved a glorious future, the cultivation of silk was carried on in what was then known as the English colonies It might have continued to flourish since then, had not England granted a charter to a joint-stock company to take African negroes to the colonies to cultivate tobacco. This new industry claimed the attention of the large land-owners, because they fancied that in it they saw more immediate profit But a few faithful women continued to raise silkworms, and to weave silk with wool for domestic wear When the war of the Revolution broke out, all else, save the necessaries of life, was neglected, and silk, with all other luxuries, almost entirely faded from the minds of the colonists.

After the close of the war, the production of cotton became general in the Southern portion of the New World Then followed its manufacture in both North and South. Then slave-labor became more general, and cotton being as easily grown as silk, and requiring less intellectual force to manufacture, it largely took the place of silk And by slow degrees, cotton, rice, tobacco, and sugar took the place of silk on all the plantations of the Southern States. Though a pound of cotton would bring but about three cents, while a pound of silk brought thirty-five to forty cents, the cotton required less skill, and would endure more abuse than the silkworms or the silk, and so it came that the silk was neglected by the large plantation-owners But as the years moved on, others, less able to hold slaves or large estates, became more interested in the production of silk, and early in the nineteenth century the *multi-cavlis* fever, as it was called, sprung up, and spread over the entire country This fever was a mere frenzy or excitement, started by unscrupulous nurserymen to sell the mulberry tree of that name So wild did the people become on this question, that single slips from ten to twelve inches long were sold at one dollar apiece. Many of the trees then planted are growing in the Southern States to-day.

At the Interstate, State, and West India Fair held in Charleston, South Carolina, in 1901 and 1902, a silk dress made from silk there produced was exhibited. The dress was one hundred and fifty years old. The silk was sent to England to be woven There are in that particular region many very old mulberry trees still growing.

The first silk-mill in the United States was erected in A. D. 1810, in Mansfield, Connecticut. Fifty or sixty years ago, there was quite an interest in the South Atlantic States in the silk business. In those days the government paid a bounty of fifteen cents on every pound of good cocoons, and one dollar on every pound of reeled silk. Then they used the Piedmontese reels, which are exceedingly simple in construction, and can be operated by any one of ordinary common sense. At that time, silk reeled on those reels brought six dollars a pound in Philadelphia. Some few years previous to the time here referred to, it is stated that scientific and learned men considered the art of reeling so very difficult a branch of knowledge to acquire, that our government was asked to endow a school with sixty thousand dollars, merely for the purpose of teaching six young men to reel silk. These young men were to attend three successive summers, four months each summer. This statement may be seen on the records of Congress. (Surely we are a progressive people.)

In 1839, a young woman went from Baltimore to Philadelphia, paid the model filature that was then operating there ten dollars for instruction, stayed there five days, and learned to reel silk. She then bought a reel, and returned home and reeled her own cocoons.

About this time silk was produced and manufactured in both the Carolinas, Georgia, Tennessee, Mississippi, Louisiana, and other states of the South. They made large quantities of silk thread, as well as cloth and hosiery; but they did not enter upon the business on a very large scale. Most persons who raised the cocoons also manufactured the silk to suit themselves, and many of the garments then woven are still cherished as heirlooms in old families of the South. Many of the mulberry trees then in use have become almost wild, for want of care and cultivation.. The silk business, like most agricultural affairs in those days, was rather an individual matter. Few, if any, of the cocoons raised were sent from the farms where they were raised and reeled till the whole work was done. But with the years the influence of slave-labor grew more and more upon the people. The masters became less inclined to labor, and the slaves became, if possible, less fitted for anything but to toil unceasingly in the dull routine of plantation-work. Their habits of life in every way unfitted them for work in silk-cocooneries, or even in silk-mills. Thus it was that in those early days of our national life, the silk industry fell into the background, and was wellnigh obliterated, save here and there, like an oasis in a desert, a few farms were given to the production of silk-worms, and a few factories manufactured both home-production and that which was brought from foreign countries.

When at last the long-agitated question of slavery reached the climax, and the tocsin of civil war burst upon the ears of the American people, the agricultural interests of the South were disrupted, as also the manufacturing interests of the North, as they looked to the cotton-fields of the South to feed their factories.

At this time in our national history there was a duty of fifteen per cent on all raw or reeled silk brought into this country This rate of duty continued till some time after the close of the Civil War.   Then all duty was removed from raw silk, and reeled silk was invoiced as raw silk, and so continues to the present, so that there is no duty on silk imported, unless it be *fully* manufactured.   Reeled silk is only twenty-five per cent manufactured, but comes in free, as though it were not twisted at all (See the monthly reports of raw silk in the American Silk Journal, published in New York)

In 1880, in Philadelphia, Pennsylvania, The Woman's Silk-Culture Association of the United States was incorporated, and placed under the able management of Mrs. John Lucas Through the efforts of this society, much good was accomplished by awakening an interest in silk-culture, both among the producers and also with the government officials The association sent out thousands of mulberry trees and cuttings to twenty-eight different states. They also freely distributed eggs, and literature giving instruction in the silk business. They had made three different kinds of silk-reels, and on them taught many young women how to reel silk From the report of the first decade of their existence as a society the following statements are quoted:—

"We have bought, raised, and reeled 12,000 pounds of cocoons, have made 2,000 yards of silk dress-goods; have sold 1,500 pounds of reeled and raw silk; have made forty silk United States flags; and have made dozens of silk handkerchiefs, fringes, ribbons, brocaded velvets, trimmings, sewing-silk, etc. Seventeen of these flags we presented to the Central and South American governments. We presented to Mrs. James A. Garfield the first silk dress made from silk raised by our association. We have sent exhibits of our work, reels, and reelers to almost every large state and agricultural fair held within the last decade. We sent a very large exhibit to the fair held in the city of London, England, a few years ago. We also held in Philadelphia two of the largest silk fairs held in any country in the world. We have distributed hundreds of ounces of eggs, thousands of trees and cuttings of the mulberry, and thousands of tracts and pamphlets on silk literature. . . . We have tested in every practical way all the different kinds of the silk-worm family and their foods, etc., and thousands of pounds of cocoons. We also sent one of our improved reels to Smyrna, in Turkey. And all this, without any member of the association receiving one cent for their time or service, and that, too, with the very limited amount received from the United States government. All the various flags, dresses, etc., presented have been paid for from the funds of the association, and not from the government funds."

A detailed account of profits and expenses of this association is also given, but want of space in this book forbids its insertion.

Just as this body of women were beginning to feel that with the continued aid of the government for a few years, they would see the silk-producing business of this country fixed on a permanent basis, the Fifty-first Congress of the United States refused to longer aid this special branch of agricultural industry, and all appropriation of funds came to a sudden end. Not only this, but it was then decided that the silk department, which hitherto had been carried on in the Agricultural Department in Washington, should be at once closed.

All through those years, while the Woman's Association was laboring to establish this great textile industry for the good of the whole country, the silk manufacturers were as faithfully working to keep it out, lest the price of the raw material be raised They opposed every measure that pointed to the possibility of a supply of silk being produced from our free soil, and chose rather to trust to the supply from European and Asiatic markets. By importing silk that was twenty-five to thirty-five per cent manufactured, as raw material, they saved to themselves about eight million dollars annually. But, let it be known that this large sum belonged to the government, and should have been paid as other import duties were, and are.

Another very potent reason why Congress at that time refused to aid this industry was, that the managers of the silk bureau at Washington had for some years been asking a very large appropriation to keep open a special silk bureau in the Agricultural Department. At last they came before Congress with a request for an annual appropriation of one hundred and fifty thousand dollars. They presented to Congress the necessity of maintaining most elaborate details of service, and a complication of offices that Congress could not see any need for, and consequently they refused to grant so large an amount, and the department refused to take any less, and so the conclusion of the whole matter was that the silk bureau at Washington was closed. The market for cocoons was no more, and what eggs of the silkworm were then on hand were scattered freely to all who sent for them. Those who received eggs were informed that there would no longer be a market in Washington for cocoons, nor was it likely there would be again for years in the United States.

The Woman's Association at Philadelphia was forced by this action to suppress all further efforts, as they were unable to bear the whole burden, and thus failed to obtain any further aid from the government.

The twenty-eight states that had planted trees, hoping soon to be self-supporting in the silk business, when the trees had attained sufficient growth, became discouraged, and turned their cocooneries to other purposes, while their mulberry groves were either neglected or hewed down for fuel.

This action of the silk manufacturers and the silk bureau at Washington, on the one hand, and the authorities at Washington on the other, disrupted the whole silk business, and for a time served to restrain successful effort in the silk business

This state of affairs came about just as San Diego became interested in silk-culture, and throughout the past decade, the same conditions existing (i. e, no market for cocoons), has proved the greatest barrier to the silk business. But amid all these seeming discouragements, the fact remains that the residents of Southern California are in possession of the finest country on the face of the globe for the production of the silkworm, as well as its best and choicest food, the mulberry tree.

But to look back over those years mentioned as to the work in the East, we must recount very briefly what was going on in California. Long before the Woman's Association was thought of in the East, M. Prevost, a Frenchman and silk-culturist, came to California He wrought a good and noble work in the northern and middle portion of the state, by demonstrating what might be accomplished here in the silk business, as compared with France. He asserted that one person here could do as much as seven or eight persons in France, in caring for worms. This, he said, was owing to the better climate, the more healthy worms, and the better food, as well as the manner of feeding. Worms raised in our healthful climate do not require such constant care as in other countries. This man was the real pioneer of silk-culture in California. He did much to encourage silk growing and manufacture for a number of years. He wrote, and talked, and labored very enthusiastically, and accomplished much more than at first he dared to hope for. Full of hope for the future of this great industry, he went back to France to secure a large invoice of the choicest eggs to be had there. But, alas! he was taken sick there, and died. And thus it happened that the silk business was, as it were, left without a head, and the attention of horticulturists was diverted to other channels of profitable labor in California.

At that time cocoons sold in France for $1.30 to $2.30 a pound. M. Prevost had in one mulberry orchard twenty-five thousand trees, and he, during one season, raised one hundred thousand silkworms without any assistance.

Joseph Newman also did much in those early days to seek to establish the silk business permanently. He tried faithfully to get the attention of Congress on this subject, and to show them where they showed great injustice to the people by passing a law allowing reeled silk to be

imported as raw material, and hence free of duty,
while they imposed a duty of sixty per cent
ad valorem on fully manufactured silks Not
only was reeled silk admitted as raw silk, but
manufacturers sent over to foreign countries their
own employees and had them *re-reel* the silk
which they called raw silk. The operation of re-
reeling silk brought it a step nearer complete
manufacture, so that it should be charged thirty-
five instead of twenty-five per cent duty. Instead
of this, however, the silk manufacturers gave this
another name,—viz., *filature* silk,—and then
imported it *free of all duty*.

At this time California was becoming quite
interested in silk-culture. The manufacturers
did not want success in this branch of industry,
and fought against it by arguing that it was best
to let the millers pierce all the cocoons raised, so
that they could only be made into spun silk. To
work out this scheme, they offered six dollars an
ounce for silk-eggs, and then destroyed the eggs,
so as to crush out this great industry, if possible.

These few facts are cited from the records of
the doings of Congress during its fiftieth session,
merely to show to those who are interested in this
business WHERE the trouble lies, and *why* silk-
producing has never gained a foothold in the
United States.

In 1869, Joseph Newman produced one hundred and thirty pounds of reeled silk, which was then worth sixteen dollars a pound. Of this he manufactured two flags twenty by thirty-six feet. One he presented to the state at Sacramento, and the other to the government at Washington, D. C.

At this time the reputation of California silk-eggs had gone abroad, and the French silk-producers contracted for about twenty thousand ounces of silk-eggs produced in California, but the Franco-German War broke out just at that time, and so disrupted all industries in those countries that the order was annulled.

Joseph Newman did much to encourage the silk business in our Golden State, but he made one grave—very grave—mistake when he advocated the cultivation of the wild silkworm. Silk made from those insects is of little or no real value.

About this time the State Board of Silk-culture was organized in this state, and did very good work on certain lines. They sent out many pages of literature, instructing the people in the art of silk-culture and planting trees, etc. They also gave instruction in reeling silk to those who wished to learn. The state had made an appropriation for the encouragement of silk-culture, and out of this fund reels were purchased and instructors employed; but no charge was made to those who learned to reel. They compiled statistics, and showed by them that California could produce millions of dollars' worth of silk every year, if only the people were properly instructed. They show us in their published literature that our nation acted unfairly in supporting training-schools for fitting soldiers and sailors to protect ·our country, while they so sadly neglected to establish schools of instruction in this great industry, which might prove a very important factor in developing our internal wealth as a nation, for it cannot be denied that wealth is the strength of every nation, state, or association. There was not then, is not now, and never has been, a national school of instruction in the art of silk-culture in the United States. In this one thing our nation falls behind any of the large silk-producing countries of the civilized world.

This State Board of Silk-culture, while not doing all that a larger and practical experience would have enabled them to do, yet they kept alive a great interest in the silk business for a few years. They offered premiums for the best cocoons, both to children and adults, and in this movement they were joined by the Woman's Silk-culture Association of the United States at Philadelphia, under the able management of Mrs. John Lucas.

Just as the State Board was beginning to realize satisfactory results from their work, and all things seemed to point to a successful establishing of the silk business in California under the assisting care of the state government, the Governor-elect refused to sign the bill passed by the legislature for the promotion of the silk industry, and thus it was that all efforts put forth to this end were lost, or at least suspended indefinitely.

As soon as this fact became known, a few energetic women in the northern portion of the state at once went to work and organized the Ladies' Silk-culture Society of California. They published circulars and sent them to all parts of the state where silk-culture had taken hold, and advertised that they would purchase all cocoons produced in the state; but the mails were slow in reaching those rural districts, and those circulars reached many sections after the mulberry trees had been uprooted and had given place to fruit trees or grain of some kind.

There were no filatures in the state, except those owned by the State Board, and kept in operation from state funds. The refusing to grant further state aid was therefore equivalent to closing the market for cocoons. With what stock remained on hand when the appropriation failed, the Ladies' Association and the State

Board kept working together, hoping that the
state authorities would yet see the advisability of
establishing silk-culture as a great industry of
the state. They labored hard, though not very
wisely, for want of practical experience. Their
selection of location for mulberry grove and place
for cocoonery was very unfortunate, as the climate
in that particular locality was not at all favor-
able to the rearing of worms. It was too cold
and foggy. The cold currents swept up from
San Francisco Bay constantly, and much care
had to be exercised in rearing the silkworms.
Moreover, they were dependent on foreigners,
who were not at all ambitious to develop any
new feature in the business. They went on in
the old European style, both as to feeding and
caring for the worms and millers. They labored
to make silk-culture entirely a cottage industry,
and opposed the idea of going into the business
on a large scale, because some speculators had
attempted to do this, and, through utter ignorance
of the requirements necessary to success, had
made utter failures They did not seem to realize
that concentrated effort on a large scale with
intelligent leadership is an absolute necessity to
produce cocoons in sufficient quantities to supply
the demand made by the manufacturers of our
own country, even though at that time there

were not half so many factories as there now are.

The failure of these large speculators is still cited as evidence against the possibility of raising silk on a large scale. Yet it is on record that in Milan, or near there, Signore Susani kept three thousand hands busy in his immense cocooneries during the season when the millers couple, and besides all these he kept 750 scientists busy examining the millers and eggs, to be sure they were free from disease.

Here in California,—yes, even in San Diego,—there is ample room for many such establishments They would add very largely to the wealth of the state and nation.

For a few years after our own state had withdrawn aid to the silk business, the Ladies' Society received from the Agricultural Department at Washington an appropriation of two thousand five hundred dollars annually. But when in 1891 Congress refused to longer give aid to this special work of development, the ladies gave up, unable to bear the burden any longer.

Since that time, several fugitive efforts have been made to develop the silk business in California, but there has been no concentrated effort in the matter, and neither state nor national aid has been given. The silk manufacturers are accumulating millions for themselves, and sending millions of dollars every year to the agricultural classes of foreign countries, for the purchase of a much poorer article of silk than they could obtain from the agriculturists of our own country.

SAN DIEGO

In A. D. 1891, a few enterprising women organized a silk society and secured the services of two skilled Japanese to instruct them in the raising of silkworms, while they managed the cocoonery (an ordinary building rented for the society). But, as a society, we had yet no mulberry trees, and the supply from other sources on which we counted proved quite insufficient for the number of worms we had hatched out. The result was, that many of the worms perished for want of sufficient food, while many of those we did rear were not at all as good as they would have been with sufficient food, all through their brief lives. However, from the few thousands we did raise, a quantity of silk-eggs was obtained, from which stock, as well as from eggs obtained from other sources, I have continued to propagate worms for a number of years. At that time we also made enough reeled, raw, and sewing-silk with cocoons to make quite a little exhibit at the Columbian Exhibition in Chicago, which attracted much attention, especially from foreigners. Our cocoons were vastly superior to most shown at that time by other silk-producing countries.

Soon after the first crop of silk had been raised, the Japanese, while fully convinced that we had the best country in the world for silk-culture, for want of means to go into the business, departed to other lines of work; and the ladies returned to the routine of every-day life. Some put in trees, but as there was no hope of very immediate returns, interest in the business almost died out.

But the writer, having full confidence in the great possibilities of our glorious land, kept on experimenting in a small way with worms, and millers, and eggs, and had as her chief reward the consciousness of doing good, by continuing to unfold new living truths from this most wonderful book of nature.

My Miniature Silk-works have long proved to be one of the chief attractions of tourists from all parts of the world.

I sent an exhibit to the Midwinter Fair held in San Francisco in 1893. In this I showed samples of fine cocoons, reeled silk from the seventh crop of worms that season; also, raw silk, sewing-silk, and a variety of silken souvenirs Some time after that I sent a small exhibit to the Mechanics' Fair (through the Carlson-Currier Company), and still later, by request of the

Southern California Railroad Company, I prepared an exhibit for the Paris Exposition, to be included in their representation of the products of California.

Samples of my silk have been taken to Europe, and examined by both foreign and our own experts, and without a dissenting voice San Diego silk has been pronounced of the best and finest quality.

At my Miniature Silk-works I continued my experiments for years. I developed splendid worms, that attained their growth in twenty-four days, and before spinning measured four inches. At one time I was three full years with living silkworms *every day*. They were continuously either hatching out or maturing. And I might have so continued ever since, if circumstances had not changed my mode of life for a time. I never found in my worms any of the diseases described in the books.

I received calls from tourists and strangers from all parts of the United States, as well as from other countries. Silk experts were always pleased to acknowledge the highest praise to our silk. I designed and made a variety of silken souvenirs, which were largely bought by numerous callers, and carried off as trophies of our sunny land's productions. These goods were also sent to all parts, by mail and express I also sent out many broods of silkworms when in the first molt. I packed in boxes with crinkled paper and fresh leaves, and they always arrived safely at their destination. I have sent them as far as Washington, D. C.

This year (1902), the interest in the silk business is much greater in all parts of the Union than I have ever known it to be. This is especially so in the Southern States The people in San Diego seem to begin to realize what undeveloped wealth is lying at their doors, and acres of mulberry trees and slips are being added to those already in The largest of these mulberry groves are owned and cared for by the following named persons: Mr. Thomas J. Swayne and wife, of Coronado; Mr. and Mrs. N. S. Casseres of National City; another party at Otay, and many others whose names do not appear.

The Theosophists of Point Loma have several acres of mulberry orchard, which, if wisely cared for, will in the near future serve to feed millions of worms.

There is ample room for all kinds of manufacture of silk in this broad land of ours. The market can never be overstocked, so long as silk, as a fabric, stands at the head of the triple crown of textile industries,—cotton, wool, and SILK.

A SILK STATION.

This year we look with ardent expectation to Congress for an appropriation to establish a silk station in San Diego.

We, as a people, need it. Not merely the people of this special locality. The people of the United States need it, and we need it right here, because this is the garden spot of the whole nation, — the place where more can be accomplished for the general good, than in any other locality in the nation. Here we have the means, through special climatic conditions, of showing to the world at large the great possibilities the American people can achieve in this, the queen of all industries. With a station here, we could educate the youth of our land, who are by nature qualified to grasp such style of instruction, to go forth into all sections of our mainland, as also into our island possessions, where they are even now asking for fuller instruction in this wonderful industry.

It is a well-known fact, that want of practical knowledge has been the cause of every failure that has occurred in silk-culture since the first cocoon was seen on the American continent. With a station here, we could generate silk-eggs by the hundreds of millions, and send them to every nation the world over. From this one source alone we could soon obtain and pour into our national treasury untold sums of gold, that would enable our rulers to build fortresses on other industrial and scientific lines, that would render our nation so strong, so thoroughly grounded on the foundation laid by our forefathers,—viz., a government of the people, for the people, and by the people,—that our enemies would quail before our national prowess, and dare not to lift up sword or battle-ax against us.

When, as is recorded of her, the little island nation Japan netted to herself eighty-five millions of dollars for silk-eggs alone in a very few years, what cannot we accomplish? What amount may not our nation justly hope to reap, with our special advantages in soil, climate, and, *above all*, with the intelligence and inventive genius of our people?

With a silk station here, we could soon send out mulberry trees and slips till the hills and plains which now greet the eyes of travelers as barren wastes, would show the riches and verdure of the "*golden*" tree; and the airy cocooneries and comfortable dwellings of busy workers would take the place of the sagebrush, and the haunts and burrows of wild beasts.

Thousands of our own citizens would seek for and establish homes on those desert plains, and add their *quota* to the taxpayers of the nation. Thousands of the best element of the working classes from foreign lands would seek and find homes in this land of freedom, where, through the influence of the higher civilization that we enjoy, they would be enabled to grasp more fully the loftier ideals of human life that we cherish.

The United States is the largest manufacturer of silks of any nation in the world. She is also the largest consumer of silk. Her territory embraces more area in latitude adapted to silk-production than any other country in the world. Then why should she not become the largest and best producer of silk?

We have all the essential elements within ourselves to carry on this great work. But we need the helping hand of the government, that the people may be educated along those special lines

National expansion has come to us as outlined on the scroll of divine prophecy. As a people, we do well to respond to its calls. San Diego, with her unrivaled harbor off the grand old Pacific, stands as the entrance to the mainland from our far-off and numerous island possessions. The call to this industry has already come from them. To respond wisely will serve to develop

them, as well as enrich the whole nation. This
is one of the reasons why we want an appropriation from Congress this year. We want to
inaugurate a system of practical education on
this special line of industry, that will prove in
its final outcome as important to the nation at
large as any of her institutions of learning, not
excepting even *West Point*.

BIBLIOLIFE

Old Books Deserve a New Life
www.bibliolife.com

Did you know that you can get most of our titles in our trademark **EasyScript**™ print format? **EasyScript**™ provides readers with a larger than average typeface, for a reading experience that's easier on the eyes.

Did you know that we have an ever-growing collection of books in many languages?

Order online:
www.bibliolife.com/store

Or to exclusively browse our **EasyScript**™ collection:
www.bibliogrande.com

At BiblioLife, we aim to make knowledge more accessible by making thousands of titles available to you – quickly and affordably.

Contact us:
BiblioLife
PO Box 21206
Charleston, SC 29413

LaVergne, TN USA
30 December 2010
210635LV00004B/5/P